OTHER BOOKS BY

How Ordinary Women Create Extraordinary Change

Take Time to Reflect: The Nourishment Journal

Keep saying "yes",
Be heard, Be seen!
Pierrette

FERRARI, FOOD OR FAMILY

WHICH ARE YOU PUTTING FIRST?

Pierrette Raymond

Ferrari, Food or Family
Which Are You Putting First?

Copyright © 2013, Pierrette Raymond.

All Rights Reserved
No part of this publication may be reproduced, stored in a retrieval system, or transmitted in any form or by any means, electronic, mechanical, photocopying, recording, scanning, or otherwise, without the expressed written permission of the author.

Pierrette Raymond
praymond@pierretteraymond.com
www.pierretteraymond.com

The individual client experiences recounted in this book are true. However, the names and certain descriptive details have been changed to protect the identities of those involved.

*To my husband Luc, our children Joshua and Briana,
thank you for being my biggest cheerleaders and supporters.
I love you all so much and I am blessed to have you in my life.
Je vous aime, jusqu'au bout!*

*A special dedication to my mother,
Lucille Beauchamp-Saudino (1947-2007),
for helping me to see what truly mattered most
through our very special time together.*

ACKNOWLEDGEMENT

Writing another book was something I had always wanted to do after publishing *The Nourishment Journal* in 2006 with my mother who was three years into her cancer diagnosis.

What I had not realized is that I would have the opportunity to spend nine of the last ten weeks of her life by her bedside before she passed away. I journaled every day about my experience with Mom, with a knowing that one day I'd share part of my journey to help inspire others to be there for their loved ones and be true to what mattered most.

When I joined a business-building program under the mentorship of Suzanne Evans (www.suzanneevans.org) and Larry Winget (www.larrywinget.com) this book came to life. Through their guidance, training and support the skeleton of the book formed, took shape and then took on a life of its own. Thank you Suzanne, Larry and the entire team, specifically Cathi Harley, Carrie Greene and Kim Wanamaker for being there to answer our many questions and coach us through our challenges. I owe you all a debt of gratitude. Thank you so very much!

A big thank you to my fellow business colleagues, the Hell Yeah Stars! Wow! What a journey it has been! I think we would all agree that the person we were at the beginning of this program is no longer the person we are today. We have grown by leaps and bounds in all areas of our lives and I personally could not have done it without you. Thank you so very much for your love, support and your friendship!

To my family and my husband's family for always being there for me, for us, during the good times and the bad. You were all so supportive of me when I was with Mom and you also continued to be during the years as I grew my home transition business alongside our 1-800-GOT-JUNK? business. I am extremely blessed to be part of such an incredible family. I love you!

To my amazing clients. Boy, have I learned a lot from you. I have always admired your courage in the face of overwhelm and you continue to inspire me as you face major life transitions. You have taught me far more than I could have ever learned on my own. Your stories are so rich, so meaningful and they mean the world to me. Thank you for being such an amazing part of my life. I am truly blessed to work with you and your families.

Lastly, to my teams, both at Moving Forward Matters and at 1-800-GOT-JUNK?. Sylvie, Lucille, Susan, Colleen, Adam, Joanne, Korey, and Davis and to all the others who have graced our businesses with your hard work and dedication. I am so honored to share you with our clients as we help them simplify their lives, move through major transitions and overcome overwhelming challenges. I'm inspired daily by your kindness; your dedication to the work that you do for others. Thank you so very much.

I truly do believe that we cannot do it alone and I'm extremely grateful to everyone, those mentioned above and those who have been my friend, my confidant, or a support to me.

Thank you so very, very much! I'm blessed to have you in my life!

CONTENTS

Introduction	11
Chapter One: What Matters Most	21
Chapter Two: You're A Mess & You Know It	35
Chapter Three: The Message In Your Stuff	47
Chapter Four: Your Purge Will Set You Free	65
Chapter Five: Letting Go to Move Forward	79
Chapter Six: A Second Chance to Let Go	95
Chapter Seven: Legacy Matters	107
Appendix: What Your Stuff Is Saying	125
Bibliography	129

INTRODUCTION

~~~~

*"Everything that can be counted does not necessarily count;
everything that counts cannot necessarily be counted."*
Albert Einstein

~~~~

"Mom? Would you like a popsicle?"

It's mid-day. The sun's rays have made their way to our side of the hospital. They shine through the hospital room window and fall gently on Mom's legs, which are covered in multiple layers of blankets to keep her warm.

She used to be so strong, fit, even a little plump, rounded in the belly like many women her age. She's young, I think. Just turned sixty. Much too young to die.

We've had some really rough mornings, mornings where I'd wonder if today would be the day. But with the sun's rays shining through and Mom's smile brightening the room, it's a good day.

It's day five of what will become my ten-week end-of-life journey with Mom.

"Mom?" I say again, taking her hand and smiling as she turns to me.

Mom is laying in her bed, slightly slumped, head elevated and plumped up with an array of pillows supporting her upper torso. I've come to master the stacking of pillows so Mom can sit comfortably and erect; a new skill that she & I will come to depend upon in the weeks to come.

She's wearing the blue hospital gown, the one that she and I have come to like the most, not like the yellow ones, which are worn and frayed. The blue ones are the best as they also bring out the color of Mom's blue eyes.

She's covered in a light top sheet, a cotton hospital blanket and a big fleece comforter.

The room is quite barren. Drab. Depressing.

On the wall at the foot of Mom's bed is her very own and quite personalized art gallery of drawings and paintings that her grandchildren have carefully created for her.

Scenic paintings of mountains and streams, with birds flying above in the painted blue sky are but one kind of masterpiece gracing Mom's wall. There's the goofy family pictures, to make Mom laugh, we say, which are slowly making their appearance in the gallery.

"Do you feel like having a Popsicle, Mom?" I ask tempting her with a special treat.

As she looks, she smiles with child-like enthusiasm.

"I'd love a popsicle."

With youthful enthusiasm of my own, I skip out of the room and make my way past the nurses' station where I give the girls a quick wave, and continue down to the small kitchen on our floor.

I open the freezer and am pleased to see that there is one Popsicle left. Smiling, I take it, snap it in two and skip back to the room, waving to the nurses again on my way by, thrilled to share this treat with Mom.

"Here you go Mom", as I pull apart her half and give it to her.

As she slowly takes her half in her small, frail hand, I can see a surge of joy come over her.

"Banana is my favorite flavor," she says, smiling.

I stop. Surprised by this news. How could I have not known that this was her favorite flavor?

Of course I know why. Being estranged from her since I was a young teenager robbed us of the simple knowings that other mothers and daughters share.

Now, for us, we were reconnecting. Rebuilding.

"Banana is my favorite too Mom!"

And it was in that moment, on that sunny Sunday morning, through this tiny little blip of time, during this very innocent and simple Popsicle moment, that the beginning of realizing the true importance of being there for who and what mattered most and honoring what was most important emerged.

Mom was dying.

Every day she faced something she could no longer do, whether it was to stand to take a walk, swallow a pill, or feed herself. My time with her put so many things into perspective. It gave me the opportunity to see what life was truly about.

This Popsicle moment would be the first of many special moments with Mom.

For ten weeks, my life stood still. Time stood still. Although everything and everyone continued to live their lives at a wickedly fast pace, I lived in a vortex where time quietly gifted me with pause, after pause, after pause.

Truth is, there was no way to escape the chipping away of the walls that Mom had put up between she and I through the many years of separation and indifference which had started long before her cancer diagnosis.

It's not like it was intentional, her apathy to not care enough to send birthday cards or call on special days. As time went by and the phone stopped ringing, the feelings of apathy become mutual.

It didn't happen overnight. It took years of crying in my husband's arms because she hadn't called to wish me a happy birthday; it took time to not care about her not caring.

Oh, I don't mean that I didn't love her or that I didn't care about her. I just stopped caring that she stopped caring. I let it go. I let her not caring go.

Until October 12th, 2003, while sitting at Mom's Thanksgiving table with my siblings on one side and my children on the other, happily laughing, eating and being the picture-perfect example of what Thanksgiving dinners are all about.

Unexpectedly, through all the laughter and joy, Mom's next words obliterate all of the years of apathy.

"I have cancer."

The laugher stops. Only silence.

My brother and sister and I look at each other. Shock. Disbelief.

Defeaning silence.

"They found a tumor on my bronchiole tube. It's inoperable", she says a-matter-of-factly.

I feel my breath, which moment ago was exhaling with laughter and joy, now forcefully taken from me in shock.

I can't breathe.

Gone is apathy.

Mom has cancer.

I inhale. A big, deep breath filled with shock, fear and sadness.

In that moment, in the span of just a few seconds, the umbilical cord that was severed 34 years ago is now reattached. We are reconnected. We are rejoined.

I breathe.

For the next five years, my relationship with my mother rebuilds. Despite living an eight-hour drive away from each other, we talk on the phone and I savor every short-and-to-the-point call I have with her. That is her style.

What neither of us knew was that fate was taking care of things. We were building a bridge, one of trust and deep connection that would eventually bring me to stay with her, by her bedside, for nine of the last ten weeks of her life.

As I sit here writing about my experience with my mother, a gorgeous and very melodious robin has perched itself on the tree branch just outside my open window.

"Hi Mom."

One of Mom's greatest loves was of songbirds. The other was of gardening. Through her two greatest passions she and I reconnected.

I took great interest in her reverence of these things; the flowers, the bountiful vegetable garden, the beautiful trees and shrubs she so masterfully cared for.

She taught me so much about the inner workings of her garden and the songs of the gorgeous songbirds. Now, every spring and summer they are like tender little love notes, surprise little love notes like the orange-crested robin perched outside my window singing happily as I write.

"Hi Mom."

She has been a constant inspiration and our experience together started me down a path of discovering what was truly important and what mattered most in my life and in the lives of others.

Seven years before her death, my husband and I moved to the nation's capital as founding franchisees of the professional removal and recycling service called 1-800-GOT-JUNK?. Although the idea of hauling away people's junk didn't seem glamorous to me, I was attracted to the potential of having a major positive impact on the environment and being of service to people who needed it most.

What I didn't foresee was my attraction to people, their stories and all of their stuff. And boy did people have a lot of stuff!

Perhaps you've seen the A&E television program "Hoarders". Let me assure you. Most people do not live in those shocking conditions but they do live in overstuffed homes with way too much stuff. In fact they are living overstuffed lives.

The reality of how much stuff people really have became very clear when I began working with families and seniors who were downsizing, organizing or moving through my company Moving Forward Matters.

Overwhelmed and stressed, my clients call upon me and my team to sort through years upon years of memories, boxes of keepsakes and yes, plenty of junk. My role is to help guide them through the letting go process so they can eliminate what is no longer needed, used or wanted, so that they keep what matters most.

For many if not most, it's not an easy process. In fact, it's extremely difficult.

They get stuck in their stuff. They get stuck in the throes of it all and what it once meant. For them, looking ahead without their stuff is frightening and downright crippling.

But there is a process. There is a step-by-step approach that I've developed that helps even in the toughest of situations, the basics for which will be shared in this book.

This book is to serve as a guide, a mentor as you look at your life through your stuff. From the stuff in your home to the stuff in your office to all the other stuff in life like your finances, your relationships, your health and well-being. This is the stuff that makes up the story of your life and for most, it's not a story you want to be writing.

Rather than living an overstuffed life, you, like many of my clients, may long to live a simpler, more organized life with time & space for who and what matters most.

That is what this book will enable you to do – simplify your life. Organize your life. Declutter your life so that you can keep what truly matters most to you, to truly be there for what is important so that you can live a life that is full, rich and abundant in all areas of your life.

Mom did have it right when she and I would talk about her journey towards her death. Being together is what mattered most. Time to create memories, to be there for each other even on the darkest of days, that is what was important.

It wasn't about cars, or luxurious homes. It wasn't about closets full of shoes or collections of designer bags.

It was about love. It was about connection. It was about being there for what mattered most.

And it was also about this moment, the moment in which I write this book. It was about her legacy and mine, all wrapped into one.

Mom gave me a very special gift, that of appreciating and honoring what was really important and what mattered most.

So if you're ready, ready to create your story, your life, and your legacy by looking at your stuff, let's go. Let's get started. I promise you won't look at your stuff the same way ever again and you will begin to create your life with what is truly important and with what matters most while you let go of the rest.

Introduction ~ 19

CHAPTER ONE

What Matters Most

*"This is as true in everyday life as it is in battle:
we are given one life and the decision is ours
whether to wait for circumstances to make up our mind,
or whether to act, and in acting, to live."*
Omar N. Bradley

"Pete! Pete!" my husband says as he runs to bring me my cell phone. "Your sister is on the phone!"

My heart plummets hard. Is this *the* call?

"Hello?" I say, my voice trembling.

"Pete. Mom had a stroke." I feel myself go weak. "It doesn't look good", she says with a deep sadness in her voice.

"What do you mean? Is she ok?" I knew she wasn't. I knew this was it. It was the beginning of the end. Mom was going to die.

"No", my sister replies. "She's not ok Pete. She's not ok at all."

Like the moment at Mom's Thanksgiving dinner table five years ago, I can't breathe. My breath is gone and I double over in pain.

I am in the parking lot, on a warm and breezy June day. I'm standing on the highest point of the parking lot overlooking the majestic view of Montreal at St-Joseph's Oratory, a magnificent church known for its pilgrimage of the sick. We are visiting the church to pray for Mom and my husband's sister who is battling her own fight with cancer.

An incredible sadness overcame me. I had just left Mom less than 24 hours ago and my promise to her would be broken. I promised I'd be there. I promised I'd be with her until the end.

Instead, I was in Montreal. Ten hours away at a church.

Moments before my sister's fateful call, I was praying. I was praying hard that Mom would die peacefully, in her sleep, letting the pain of her cancer-ravaged body die while she transitioned to Heaven.

I also prayed hard that I'd make it back to her in time. I wanted so badly to keep my promise to her and be there with her until the very end.

Being with Mom was not about her dying. It was about her living and making every moment we had together count.

When Mom was taken to the hospital nine weeks earlier, she had gone seeking relief of the excruciating pain that she was in. The cancer had taken its toll on her. What we didn't know was that Mom would be in the hospital until she took her last breath.

The first day of my ten-week journey with her was two days after she was admitted. I remember realizing how important it was for me to be with her, in case these were her final days. I had to be with her. I longed to be with her.

Upon arriving at the hospital, I couldn't believe how frail Mom looked. Although I had seen her just a few weeks ago, the dramatic change to her body was crushing.

She *was* dying.

That was when I made the decision, the commitment to stay with her until the very end. I decided I would not leave her. I would stay and care for her and make sure that whatever time she had left would be as good as it could be.

Little did I know that that decision would have me with her for nine weeks, by her side, sleeping in her hospital room, eating hospital food, showering, doing my laundry, living at the hospital, in a city eight hours away from my husband, our two children and our two businesses.

In those nine weeks, although I missed my family and my businesses took a major beating, I knew there was nowhere I would rather be than with Mom.

Mom was dying and I was living fully.

It was also in those moments with Mom that I realized that nothing was more important than being there for our loved ones. Nothing was more important than showing up and giving of oneself to help someone we care about make it through challenging times.

I also realized that no stuff, no physical stuff could ever take the place of the deep and meaningful joy that being there for a loved one could bring. It was not about the stuff. It was never about the stuff.

I wanted Mom to feel love, deep, deep love. I wanted her to know that no matter what would happen, she was important and she mattered.

"I'm going to stay Mom", I told her, two days into what was supposed to be my short stay with her. "I'm going to stay with you. I know how much you hate being in the hospital alone so I'm going to hang out with you. Is that ok?"

I remember the surprised look on her face. "You are?" she said, longing for what I was saying to be true.

"I am Mom. I've made the arrangements and I'm going to stay. I'll get everything organized and set up for the businesses and I'll be with you until, well, until…." I said my voice trailing off. "I want to be here with you."

Mom smiled. She was relieved. She would not be alone.

I kept my promise. I kept it until the last week of her life. Until I gave my power away and didn't listen to what was really important, to what really mattered.

Up until this point, I had made the decision to be with Mom. I was living my life honoring what was most important even if it meant making sacrifices along the way.

I was showing up for what truly mattered despite being criticized by my siblings for not going back home and being there for my husband and children, and my businesses.

I had made the promise to Mom that I would stay with her until the end and I intended on keeping my promise. Not for me, but for her.

I kept that commitment and promise until I gave my power away.

Four days before Mom had her stroke, my in-laws decided they would visit my husband and children back home on the weekend. Father's Day was approaching and my wedding anniversary was just a week away. I had put so much strain on my husband and my children that I wrestled with continuing to put Mom first and them second. Maybe I could go back home for the weekend for respite and spend time with them. Maybe it would be ok to leave for a couple of days.

I struggled and fought awful thoughts with every side of the decision. No matter what I decided, someone would be upset that I would not be there with them.

Two days before I left, I told Mom I'd be leaving for the weekend. I needed to put my husband and the kids first for just a couple of days. I knew she was terribly upset that I was leaving.

I did my best to comfort her and make our last two days together as good as I could. I painted her finger and toenails. I read to her and held her hand when she was awake and at night I moved my cot next to her bed so that I could hold her hand while she and I slept.

I wrestled with every breath that I was making the right decision, knowing that I could miss her passing and break my promise to her.

On my last day with her, I gave her a pin-on angel. She was pretty, gold-covered and shimmered with crystals on her head, wings and body.

"I'll always be with you Mom", I whispered as I pinned the angel to the cuff that was protecting Mom's elbow from bedsores. "She'll watch over you for me while I'm away."

When it was time to leave, I fought back the tears but it didn't help. They flowed as I kissed her and told her how much I loved her. We looked in each other's eyes, a look that said we both hoped it would not be the last time we would see each other. We both cried and I didn't want to go. I didn't want to let her go. I kissed her often and told her that I loved her. I told her how much I loved being with her and how grateful I was for the time we had together.

I kissed her one last time, told her that I loved her and left.

As I walked out of the hospital room, the room that I had called home for so many weeks, I felt so empty, so lost, so broken. After committing to be with Mom until the very end and promising her that I would stay, I was leaving.

I knew what my priorities were and I showed up for Mom in every way that I could. I was there for her when others were not. I stayed by her side day after day, night after night. I became her primary caregiver and the nurses turned to me for guidance after I had created systems and procedures to help Mom be comfortable in her depleting body.

I did my very best and I was honored to be there.

And then…the moment that my cell phone rang in the parking lot at the church, I gave my power away.

My heart ached to be with her. I wanted so badly to get on the next plane and get right back to her, to be with her by her side, holding her hand, reading angel passages to her, singing to her and comforting her.

But I didn't. Instead, I stayed with my family back home.

It was clear from my mother's common-law partner that after Mom died there would be no room for me in their home. Mom wanted her body cremated with no service or funeral.

My sister was renovating her kitchen and said she would spend time on her project when Mom died. My brother told me he'd go fishing.

And I would be left alone.

When we left the Oratory that day, as we pulled away from the majestic church where I had prayed to be back with Mom, I had the uncontrollable urge to call her. If I wasn't going to be with her, I would settle and call her. I would say good bye and I would let fate take its course.

We were eight of us in our van. My husband was driving. My father-in-law was in the passenger seat. My mother-in-law, sister-in-law and her husband were in the middle seat and I was in the backseat with my daughter on one side and my son on the other.

I was weeping. I was shaking. Mom was going to die. I had to tell her that I was with her and that it was ok for her to go.

"Hello – this is Pierrette", I told the nurse who instantly recognized my voice. "Can you put the phone to Mom's ear so that I can…I can say…good bye", I wept.

"I will do that Pierrette. One moment."

I could hear her placing the phone to Mom's ear. I couldn't hear Mom breathing but I felt her presence with me. I wanted her to know that I was with her. She had to know that I was with her.

"Mom?", I said trying so hard to be strong. "Mom", I repeated. "I love you. I'm so sorry I'm not there with you. I'm sorry you had a stroke. I want you to know that I love you and that it's ok for you to go. It's ok Mom. It's ok to go."

I couldn't help but cry. This was my last good bye and I had to let her know how much I was going to miss her and how much I loved her.

"I love you Mom. I love you so much! I will miss you and I will always keep you in my heart", I said pausing, waiting for her to answer. But she couldn't. "I love you Mom."

As I pressed "END" on the phone, I sobbed. I never felt so alone.

We made the drive back home to Ottawa, a two-hour drive that seemed like an eternity. I held onto the phone, waiting for it to ring with the news that Mom had passed away.

My husband and his family made dinner and continued with their visit. There was nothing they could do. There was nothing I could do.

So we waited.

I checked in on Mom every two hours, calling the nurses who were now my confidants and friends after being there with them for nine weeks. We got to know each other well, sharing stories about our families while I became a permanent resident on their floor.

"How is Mom doing?" I'd ask, every time I'd call.

"It could be any time, Pierrette", they would answer.

That *any time* lasted a week.

Day after day I was told that Mom would die 'today'. Day after day I'd call in for reports, every two hours, to see how she was doing, to see if there was hope for me to go back to be with her. Day after day, I suffered alone, longing to be with her, to comfort her, to hold her hand.

I did the rosary with Mom several times while the nurses held the phone to Mom's ear.
The nurses knew that I would be there if I could. But why wasn't I there?

Twelve hours before Mom died I realized that I had given my power away.

With all my being, I wanted to be with Mom. That was where I had been for nine weeks and I made a promise that I would be with her until the very end. Why wasn't I on a plane to be with her?

It was in that moment that I decided to book a flight and get back to being with Mom. No matter what would happen now, I was taking my power back and I was going to be there for her.

I called the hospital and did the rosary with Mom one last time. I recorded it this time. I don't know why I did but I did. I told Mom how much I loved her and that I was coming to see her in the morning. I told her that I would be with her soon and that I loved her very much.

Before heading to bed, I set my alarm for 4:30 am for my flight back to Mom.

At 12:05 am on June 18th, 2007, I was awakened by something; something on the radio woke me, although the radio wasn't on. I thought of Mom.

"Are you ok Mom?" I thought to myself.

Ten minutes later, the phone rang. It was the nurse.

"Pierrette. Your Mom passed away", she said saddened by the news she was giving me.

"What time did she die?", I asked holding back the tears.

"I checked in on her at midnight and she was alive. When I came back in, she was gone."

"What time is it?"

"It's 12:10 am"

"Thank you. Thank you for taking such good care of her", I said as the tears began to fall. "I appreciate all that you have done."

"You were great for your mother Pierrette. She was lucky to have had you here. I'm really sorry for your loss."

"Thank you", I said as I hung up.

I made the phone calls to my sister, my brother and my father.

I then sobbed in my husband's arms while I listened to the recording of the rosary I said with Mom just a few short hours ago. At the end of the recording, I told Mom how much I loved her and how much I missed her. I sobbed with deep, deep sorrow.

Before I headed back to bed, I turned off the alarm that I had set on my cell phone for my flight. I wouldn't be going home until I was told it was ok to do so now that Mom was gone.

At 4:30 am, my alarm went off.

"What?" I thought to myself. "I had shut off the alarm."

I took the phone into my hands and checked the alarm and sure enough, it was on 'off'.

I put the phone down wondering what was going on. A minute later, the alarm went off again and the time on my phone read 4:30 am. Surprised, I checked my alarm and again it was on 'off'.

Throughout my time with Mom, we talked about the afterlife. We talked about what could possibly come next. Neither of us could be certain of course but I believed that Mom's spirit would continue to live once she had left her body.

I wanted so much for her to believe that too.

I often asked Mom to give me a sign that she had made it ok after she had passed. We had been reading books by James Van Praagh and Sylvia Browne and we wondered if all of their stories could possibly be true.

So I asked Mom to let me know, to give me a sign, that she had made it ok when she had left this physical world to transition into the next one.

When my husband and I realized what was happening with my alarm we both gave thought that it was Mom giving me a sign that she was ok and that she had made it safely Home.

I share this story with you for a few reasons. The first is to tell you how terribly sad I was that I gave my power away after being so committed to Mom and my promise to her.

When I found out that Mom had a stroke, I should have simply got on the next plane to be with her. It is what I longed to do, it is what I wanted to do. But because of what my family was going to do, and because of Mom's final wishes, I held back and didn't do what I felt was important to do.

Please know that I'm a firm believer that things happen for a reason and that the experiences we go through are here to teach us and allow us to grow. They are also here to allow us to learn from them so we don't make the same mistakes again.
If I could go back, I would make a different choice. But I'm also ok knowing that I was not meant to be with Mom when she passed despite my promise and commitment to her. I've reconciled that regret and want to offer the learning as you go through the book, making decisions about what is truly important in your life.

You will be faced with deciding what to keep and what to let go. You will be asked to make decisions that are based on what is truly important to you and what matters most.

Having a clear and focused idea on what you want in your life coupled with what you currently have will allow you to move through the process we are going to go through together in this book.

I suffered a great deal the entire week after Mom's stroke because I didn't do what I knew I should do, what was most important to do. I gave my power away thinking I'd be left alone after she died.

If there is ever a great lesson I carry, that is the biggest of them all. And I share it with you so that you can check yourself in your moments of doubt and ask yourself what is really and truly important. With that in mind, how will you decide?

Even though I wasn't with Mom physically at the end, I was with her, with every inch of my being. I had not left her side the day I walked out of the hospital room. I called her. I spoke to her. I said the rosary with her. I prayed for her. I was with her.

I showed up for her. I showed up for her because she mattered most, because she was dying, and my time with her was limited.

One of the reasons I am writing this book is because of the experiences I had with her. I got so very clear on what was really important in life – what 'stuff' was just stuff and what stuff really mattered.

The people that were there for me to love and support me have earned my deepest gratitude because they showed up for me when I needed them most.

Our priorities change. They ebb and they flow. But one thing never changes. That is the love we have for the most important people in our lives and that is what really matters.

It's not about the stuff that fills our homes, or the cars that we drive, or the restaurants in which we eat.

It's about being there for each other, for the people that are most important to us. To prioritize our lives based on what is really and truly important and live our lives accordingly, showing up and being there with grace, compassion, kindness and love.

It's not about the Ferrari in the driveway.

It's not about the food we spoil ourselves with.

It's about the people that we love and creating lasting and loving memories to fill a lifetime.

Mom has been a guiding light in my life. My experience with her has made me appreciate all that is truly real and special in my life.

It's now your turn.

What will you decide?

It's your stuff. It's your story. It's your life.

CHAPTER TWO

You're A Mess & You Know It

~~~~
*"Contentment is not the fulfillment of what you want,
but the realization of how much you already have."
Anonymous*
~~~~

There's a knock on the front door. You're not expecting anyone. Who could it be?

You make your way to the entrance, almost tripping over the shoes your teenager left on the floor. You open the door and you see me smiling back at you.

"What are you doing here?" you ask, wondering what I could possibly be doing at your door.

"I'm here to do a walk-thru of your home", I say, smiling.

Your heart drops.

"You're here to do what?" you ask feeling a sense of panic rising.

"I'm here to do a walk-thru of your home."

You've heard about me and how I help families and individuals who are living overstuffed lives but you never expected me to show up at your front door.

"I'm here to look around, to see every room, every space, every closet, and cubbyhole," I continue. " May I come in?"

You frantically do a mental scan of each room in your house and know there's no way you want me to do a walk-thru now. Not *now*. There's just way too much stuff and much of it is out of place, it's unorganized and well, it's just a mess. It definitely is not the picture of you and your life that you'd want me to see.

I stand at the door, smiling warmly at you. "Will you let me in?"

~~~~~~~~~~~~~~~~~~~~~~~~~~~~

How are you feeling? Relieved maybe that no one is at your door asking to do a walk-thru of your home.

If you need to, take a deep breath. Relief. Smile.

So no one is at your door, right? But let's play just the same ok? Let's have some fun with this.

I'll admit. When someone comes to my door unexpectedly I too do a mental scan of my home, the front entrance especially and wonder what can they see. Are the shoes put away? Are the coats hung in the closet? Are the dog leashes out of sight?

I am the first to admit that I don't like unexpected company. I cringe when the doorbell rings and I have to answer the door. I always find myself scanning the areas people will see, picking things up that may be lying around before I even open the door.

It does happen. I'm human and my life is pretty full too.

But I have learned a lot in the past thirteen years and my home is just one area that I've focused on when it comes to prioritizing and living with what is most important.

You also know that the time spent with my mother had a profound impact on how I view the stuff in my life.

Through my work, especially with my two businesses as one of the founding franchise partners of 1-800-GOT-JUNK? and the owner of Moving Forward Matters, a home transition business, I've helped thousands of people simplify their lives, downsize their property, let go of what is not important in all areas of their lives.

The result? Abundance!

Truly! Having less stuff opens up our lives for what matters most, what we cherish and love and creates a life of abundance in all areas, including relationships, finances, health and well-being.

So let's play with this initial idea that I came to your home to look around and assess your life based on the stuff you have in it. How would you react? Better yet, how would you feel?

My clients invite me into their homes and offices all the time. Although they feel very uncomfortable and worry that I am judging them harshly because of the condition their home or office is in, it is not my role to judge or criticize. I am there to help and support them, not condemn them.

I know that it's not easy to get to a point in our lives where we begin to admit to ourselves that our life is not where we thought it would be, nor what we want it to be.

We often think that our lives are so full, and yet, we often feel so empty.

We've worked long and hard most of our lives to get all that we have and yet, when we look at what is in our homes, all that we have around us, we can feel very empty.
I'm no stranger to this myself. I too found myself wondering, "How did I end up here?"

Looking at myself, twenty-five years ago, coming out of high school, university-bound with all the dreams for my life in place, I thought that by the age of thirty I'd have all the financial pieces of my life in place and that by the age of forty, I'd be wealthy. I'd be living in a big house, driving a nice car, and I'd have plenty of money in the bank. I'd be travelling around the world with my husband and my family and I'd be living comfortably with very few worries.

But as you may know, life often has its own plans and you simply find yourself going with the flow of things, doing the best that you can with what you know, and what you have, at that time.

I didn't plan on not finishing my degree because my parents separated during my last year of university. I didn't plan on my father being suicidal and my saving his life. I didn't plan on moving to Ottawa to start a franchise business that would eventually grow to be over seven figures.

I also didn't plan on my mother having cancer and my spending nine of the last ten weeks of her life by her bedside making sure they were the best days she could hope for.

And I definitely didn't plan on my daughter having to endure four years of being bullied and ostracized, which has now led to her recovery from depression.

Those are just some of the things I didn't plan and I'm sure your list is just as long as mine.

On the flip side, a lot of what I did plan happened just about the way I had planned it. I planned on being married young. I planned on being a mother, having two children by the age of 28. I planned on owning a house and raising my family in a loving home. I planned on being a great mother, studying what parenting experts offered as their best advice and adapting it to suit my family and my goals. Those were the great plans. And they worked out well!

I did end up with a big house, a nice car (or two), and a lot of money in the bank.

On the outside, it looked like I had reached many of my goals and that I was living the good life.

Unfortunately, inside though, I wasn't feeling that way.

I was feeling empty, like something BIG was missing. And it wasn't stuff that I was missing. We had plenty of that.

It was the other stuff; the stuff of fulfillment, the stuff of feeling full inside, of feeling great about oneself and feeling a sense of contentment that comes when you know you are doing what is important and what matters most.

That was the stuff that was missing. And I didn't know how to find it. I didn't realize it was not something to be found. It was something that came to you.

Someone is at the door again. Are you ready to answer?

Let me ask you – what if this were a true story? What would you do if I or someone else would come to your door unexpectedly and ask to do a walk-thru of your home?

I do know, that for some, you wouldn't have a problem with it. Your home is kept neat and tidy and you are very well organized. For you, it wouldn't take much to straighten a few things and you'd gladly let me in.

I also know that for many, you would slam the door in my face and run around like a crazy person trying to tidy the house for me to come in.

You'd yell to your kids to come help you. You'd grab things and hide them in places you think I wouldn't look. And you'd think to yourself how did you let things get this way.

Well, truth is. Many of us are a mess and we know it. And we know others who are too.

We may be living a life that is extremely full and yet, on the inside, we are feeling quite empty.

Sure we don't show it on the outside but behind closed doors things are much different.

When I was seven years old, I remember feeling ashamed by our house. The house was painted white with wood siding. The brown and orange trim was peeling and it looked uncared for.

We had bluish-green shag carpet inside and the house just looked old.

To me it shouted that we were poor and I cringed at the idea of having friends over because I didn't want them to see how poor I thought we were.

That was the movie playing in my head. I was ashamed and I internalized it as not being good enough.

My parents would attest if they could that we were not poor. They had limited resources for major renovations but they did find a way to fix up the house. And in fixing up the house, they fixed the way I felt about myself.

With the house now renovated with new siding, a new kitchen and new carpeting, I felt so proud of the home we lived in. I felt rich!

What I once felt as shame was now replaced with pride. I wanted my friends to come visit. I wanted them to see how well-off we were.

Looking back, I can see how my self-worth increased as the appearance of the house changed. I had not realized that until now, until writing this book.

This is quite the revelation for me to admit. In my journey to getting to where I am now, I have to confess that I made sure that my husband and I had a house that was nice, that looked great, and that showcased our success so that our children would feel good about themselves and the lives that they had.

My childhood experience of feeling poor because of the house we lived in and then feeling rich after it was renovated has carried itself through to my adulthood. I strived to ensure we had a nice home, a home of prestige so my children could feel good about themselves.

I know it's ludicrous but it is the experience that I had. And it has stayed with me all of this time.

That is just one consequence of feeling less than good enough through my parents' stuff. It has most certainly come through in other areas of my life too.

From struggling financially to make us look wealthy to my eating disorder and over-exercising to be thin, I have experienced the damaging effects of striving to be what society depicts as successful.

I've also experienced the deep overwhelm of having too much stuff; a cluttered garage, a messy basement, and overstuffed closets.

I understand what it is like and I understand how much of a mess it can all be, especially as a woman, as an entrepreneur, as a mother and wife.

It's a lot. It's too much.

With our untidy home, came our messy life.

But all that has changed for me now. From the life-changing experience that I had with my mother, to the work that I do with clients, putting things back in order, physically and figuratively, is something that is part of my daily life.

It is also extremely apparent to me that our physical stuff mirrors all the other stuff in our lives.

I've seen it in myself and I've seen it in my clients. Having a lot of physical clutter creates turmoil in our finances, our relationships and in our health.

So, let's take a look at some of your stuff. When it comes to your finances, you may owe more than you would like. Your credit cards may not ever be paid in full. You have little or no savings, much less anything put aside for your later years. You have purchased things that made you feel good at the time, but now they lay collecting dust, never being used.

You've put on extra weight and you've added bad habits to your day. Too much sugar, not enough exercise, bad bedtime routine, and sleepless nights may be part of your daily routine.

You're stressed about work and all that you have to do. You wish you could change jobs or start your own business, or simply just have more time off to do the things you want to do.

You have kids who live at home who don't help enough around the house. Their rooms are hardly ever tidy and they have activities that keep you out on most nights and weekends.

Your parents are aging and they call upon you for errands, to do things and to just talk on the phone, something you don't necessarily like to do when all you want to do is rest and watch tv.

You're always on the go and rarely take the time to take care of you. You can't remember the last time you went for a massage or took a hot bath by candlelight. You want nothing more sometimes than to pack your bags and go away for a week on a secluded island so you can be alone. Just the thought of some peace and quiet makes you smile.

And the list goes on.

Messy desk. Dirty car. Cluttered garage and basements.

All you want is a magic wand and the fairy godmother to come make it all neat, tidy, organized and better. Boy, would that feel great!

But that won't happen. There is no magic wand and you will be stuck in your mess unless you do something now to change it.

It's time for you to change it. And that's key. You have time to change it.

I'd like to repeat that. You have *time* to change it!

Working with seniors offers me a perspective I don't get from working with others. It's like having a crystal ball that lets me peek into the future of what could be.

So when I say you have time to change it, you *really* do have time to change it!

Eddy is our friend. He is someone we met over ten years ago when he and his wife were our neighbors. My son mowed their lawn in the summer and shoveled their driveway in the winter. We were close and once his wife died, we took him under our wing to help him get through his really dark days.

For several years, we ran his errands, cooked meals for him and spent time with him. On the outside, he looked like he was doing ok. He looked like he was happy.

Unfortunately, he wasn't.

He was extremely lonely and he missed his wife. On the outside, he made everything appear to be ok. On the inside, he was living a very empty life.

In the summer of last year, we were hit with a very sad and unexpected reality. Eddy was broke. He had used up all of his savings, maxed out his credit and was now facing bankruptcy.

Before we found out the truth, Eddy had lied to us and told us that he had been defrauded of an extensive amount of money. We were told that he'd have the money returned to him by his banking institution but it was all a lie. For four months, we lent Eddy money to pay his rent and purchase food and medications. We never suspected that he had run out of money.

It wasn't until the day we set up a meeting with his banking officer that the truth was revealed to us.
Eddy was bankrupt. And we were his only source of family and friends, so we did what most people encouraged us not to do. We took him into our home to live with us.

He stayed with us for five months and recently, moved into a small basement apartment where he is rediscovering being independent while "filling himself up" with friendship and gratitude, rather than all the wrong stuff.

Eddy would like others to learn from his mistakes. He wants to urge us to pay attention to what is really important and not let irresponsible choices, despite being made in times of loneliness, sadness or grief, ruin our friendships, our family and potentially our lives.

As you can imagine, through my work, I've seen a lot of stuff. I've seen more than the average person will see in their entire lives. And our stuff is awfully revealing!

Want to know what your stuff is saying about you? Yes, that is what I said. What your stuff is saying about you.

I'd like you to know that your stuff, all of your stuff, is speaking loud and clear. It's actually saying more than you know, and it will reveal a lot about what you may be feeling, experiencing and going through that has kept you stuck, feeling bogged down or even, feeling quite empty.

You may be feeling that your life is overstuffed and you're waiting to find the answer when in fact, the answer will come to you when you go to it.

I kow that it's not always easy but it truly is the place to start.

In fact, you have to go to it. You have to go to your stuff.

So, here's your chance, a chance to experience your life in a whole new way. One that will reveal what is holding you back and keeping you stuck by highlighting what is truly important and what is cluttering up your life.

Here's your chance to create the life that you want with what is most important.

If you're ready to go, let's get started.

CHAPTER THREE

The Message In Your Stuff

"The best and most beautiful things in the world cannot be seen or even touched - they must be felt with the heart."
Helen Keller

If ever you've watched an episode of "Clean Sweep" or "Extreme Clutter" with Peter Walsh, professional organizer and clutter buster extraordinaire, you'd absolutely agree that people have way too much stuff and that their stuff says a lot about them.

Most episodes feature people living in extreme clutter. Not quite the chronic hoarding cases as seen in "Hoarders" or "Hoarding: Buried Alive", but the more-than-common way people are living in North America. There's just so much stuff.

Peter Walsh has dedicated a better part of his career, especially after being Oprah's featured organizer for years, to helping people declutter and get control of their lives. What I loved most about his books and his television shows was that it showed the real truth about our stuff. It featured the stories behind why someone kept something versus throwing it away.

My work with my clients is quite similar and the stories that come from the stuff my clients have are rich, powerful and extremely meaningful – to them. To me, it's stuff. There's no attachment, no story. To them, it's a link to their past, a loved one and a time when that item meant so much to them. And still does.

As we enter the next phase of the process we're going to go through together, I'd like you to start thinking in terms of what your stuff is saying to you and about you. You will have an opportunity to go deeper and really explore this further. For now though, begin to bring this awareness into your focus as we take the next steps.

I'd like you to imagine yourself at the very center of your home, in a room that you would consider the heart of your home; it could be the kitchen, the living room, or the dining room. It doesn't matter. Pick a room that feels like the heart of your home.

Now imagine yourself there, in that room, feet firmly planted on the floor.

Look around you. What do you see? What is around you?

Look at the walls, the floor, and the furniture. Turn slowly so you make a 360-degree turn and notice EVERYTHING in that space. Notice the walls, the flooring, and the furniture. Notice what is on the furniture, on the walls, and on the floor.

Look closely at everything in that room. Every detail is important so note it as you mentally scan the room.

As you are scanning the room and looking at all that is around you start paying attention to how you feel. How does this space and all that is in it make you feel?

Is it cluttered, unorganized, a mess?

Is the paint chipped, the carpet stained, the flooring damaged?

Does it contain some of your most prized possessions, proudly displayed and honored?

What is this room saying to you?

What is the stuff saying to you?

What is the stuff saying *ABOUT* you?

Pause. Pay attention. What is it saying *about* you?

Now mentally walk from this room to the next and stop and repeat the scan. What is in the room? What does it feel like? How do you feel in it?

Continue to do this mental walk-thru of your home until you've done every room. Take detailed mental notes and don't leave a room until you've done a complete mental scan of it.

Now, if you are feeling somewhat overwhelmed by this experience, it's ok. It's good to acknowledge things as you mentally see them so that you can take steps to change what you want to change later. And yes, I'll show you how.

For now though, this is the starting point of where you are. There is no shame in it. No guilt. It is what it is and that's where you will start.

What you have just experienced is what most of my clients experience when I first meet them. They come to me feeling overwhelmed by what their life is revealing to them, physically, financially, emotionally, spiritually and psychologically.

They want to slow the pace of their lives down to take into account what they do have and then sift through the chaos to find peace from the overwhelm. They need help to go through what is in their homes or their offices so they can downsize to what is really important and to what matters most.

It always takes being honest with where they are, what they have, why they have it and knowing that they want it to be different.

> *Tracy was a mother of two children with a third on the way. She had a lovely home and kept it very clean and organized. When she called me, she was looking for help with her basement.*
>
> *When her grandmother died, her father could not deal with the physical stuff his mother had in her home. Rather than face it, he boxed it all up, in forty-seven boxes, and labeled them "Do not open until 2020", the year his first grandchild would turn eighteen. The boxes were then stored in Tracy's basement, much to her chagrin.*
>
> *For years, the boxes reminded her of her deceased grandmother. They also weighed heavily on her conscious as she knew that what was packed in the boxes was not sorted nor dealt with.*
>
> *With a third child on the way, she wanted to transform her basement into a family room with a play area for her children.*
>
> *She agonized about opening the boxes, especially after her father had labeled them to remain sealed but she knew that she had to get through the boxes to create the family room she had envisioned.*
>
> *During our consultation, I empathized with her. She was burdened with the charge of sorting through her deceased grandmother's items long after she had passed but she knew it*

> *was time for her to unseal the boxes and move forward with her life.*
>
> *We worked together for four sessions, opening one box after another and sorting through all of the contents. We organized what she wanted to keep and donated what she didn't want but could be used by someone else. The rest was brought to the waste site.*
>
> *It was extremely difficult for Tracy when the first few boxes were opened but in a short amount of time the weight lifted and she began to embrace what was most important and what she had envisioned for her basement. Through my gentle guidance and help, and her commitment to her goal the decisions came easier and she got through the experience in a way that honored her grandmother and the love that she had for her. She also released her father from any ill feelings that she may have had.*

My experience with Tracy is a constant reminder of how precious our memories are and that to box them up and store them away is a dishonor to the ones that we love. Tracy was brave and she showed her true nature when the first few boxes were opened. It was not an easy process for her but she knew by pushing through the initial pain of it, she'd find her way. And that she did.

Today she has a beautiful playroom for her three daughters and a family room to create lasting memories for her family. And yes, there are a few of her grandmother's mementos proudly displayed in her family room for her to share with her children.

What Tracy did and what we all need to do to make changes in our lives is to take into account where we are, what is cluttering up our space (inside and out) and make a decision to go through it, one step at a time, to make it what we truly want it to be.

So let's do the walk-thru again but this time with a paper and pen. Yes, you are now going to physically do a walk-thru of your home.

Whoa! You may be thinking. That's too much!
But it isn't. You need to *see* the stuff in your life. You need to *physically* see it. And from there you'll get to *feel* it too.

I'm guessing that there are several areas of your home that have stuff in it that you haven't seen for years. I'm also going to guess that some of it you have forgotten you even had.

Why would I say that? Because I see it and live it with clients every single day.

It's stuff. It gets put away, forgotten and stored. It's not until we start going through it that we begin to see how much of it we really have.

You can say this applies to the other stuff in your life too, like your relationships, your finances, and your health. But we'll get to that a bit later.

For now, let's do the walk-thru exercise.

Grab a pad of paper and a pen and start at the heart of your home. Work your way through every room, assessing each room for what is in it, how it makes you feel and what you love/hate about it.

Use a very critical eye to look at *EVERYTHING* in every room from the floors to the ceilings, to every nook and cranny of space. It's time to get real and see your stuff.

Now go!

~~~~~~~~~~~~~~~~~~~~~~~~~~~~~~

So what did you discover?

Did you do each room, including the garage, the attic, the backyard shed? Did you also do under the stairs, the cubbyholes and the closets? Did you open your kitchen drawers, bathroom cabinets and all storage cupboards?

How much stuff do you have? How much did you not see in your mental walk-thru? Was there more than you could remember?

How do you feel?

When we complete a walk-thru with a client, our goal is to assess where they are and what we can do to help them meet their objectives to downsize their property, declutter and organize their home or complete a full home transition.

When I'm working with clients privately on a coaching level, we're doing the same thing but on a much deeper level, tackling all areas of their lives.

There is something to be said here. My team and I never judge or criticize. It's not our role. And it's not yours either.

You are not to look at your stuff, the areas of your home or the areas of your life and beat yourself up for where you are. That is not helpful nor will it get you anywhere.

Sure you can get pissed off and decide things have to change. That's good. Often it's only when we get fed up enough that we do in fact do something to change. So it's ok if you're pissed off at yourself. You'll use that energy soon!

But don't wait for a crisis please! Don't wait until something unexpected and awful happens before you are forced to make a change. Please don't wait for that.

Much of our work with seniors and their families comes at a time of crisis in their lives. There's been a fall, a critical illness, or a death. Their circumstances have changed overnight and now they are forced with having to make major life decisions in a time of great overwhelm, sorrow or grief.

Although we do a great job assisting them and helping them get through it all, we hate having to see them go through what they are going through when a lot of what we are helping them deal with could have been taken care of, sorted, dealt with earlier when the circumstances were far happier, calmer and within their control.

So please, do not wait for a crisis before taking steps to enhance and simplify your life.

Let's acknowledge where you are now and what irks you the most, what you want to change and what will make your life happier, healthier, and wealthier with less.

Now as you look at your list and the inventory you created, what message is your stuff giving? What is it saying about you?

Often we find that the stuff is saying a few things:

- Priorities of what is important aren't aligned with the stuff
- There is too much stuff
- There is stuff that has little or no value
- The stuff has taken over a space, a room, a home, a life
- Some of the stuff doesn't belong to us
- What is said to be important is buried in dusty-old boxes
- Items of great sentimental value are not properly stored & cared for
- What is known to be of great value is not professionally appraised and insured
- Etc., etc., etc.

When I had my women's self-development organization from 2002-2008, our focus was to look at all areas of our lives and do one thing, each week, to improve the quality of those areas.

These small goals that we set for ourselves created incredible momentum and change. Women were finding themselves happier, healthier, having better relationships with the people they love and their wealth began to increase.

It wasn't by chance. It was by choice.

We'd meet in-person and share our successes. When we wouldn't hit our goals, we'd re-evaluate, readjust and give it another shot.

If the goal was too big, we'd chunk it down into smaller, more achievable goals that would lead to the larger goal.

If we kept missing a goal, we'd have to be honest with ourselves and see if it was a goal that was misaligned with what was most important in our lives or if there was something keeping us stuck where we were.

And that was the key. We had to look at ourselves, be honest with ourselves and determine how important the goal was and if we were sabotaging our own success.

We never set goals to have more stuff in our lives. Our goals were about being healthier, happier, feeling less stressed, and having greater, richer experiences with the people we loved and those in our communities.

Our money goals were about getting us to a place where we didn't have to worry about money. We all wanted to be debt free, building our wealth and planning for our futures.

It wasn't about buying big screen tv's, or fancy cars or shoes. Ok, maybe for some, there were 'shoe' goals.

The point is when we aligned ourselves with what was really important in our lives our goals reflected that.

And things began to happen – we achieved our goals!!

So where does that put you today?

Where are your priorities? What is most important in your life?

Is it money? Wealth? Status?

Is it family? Fun? Friendship?

Is it having a fancy car and wearing designer clothing?

Is it traveling around the world and being care-free?

What is really important in your life will guide you in every decision that you make.

And that's where I see many people making really bad decisions. Decisions that hurt what they say is the most important thing in their life – their loved ones.

A few years ago, I conducted a survey. I surveyed over 1000 women. I asked them what was most important in their lives. You can probably guess what they said.

Yes – their family.

My next question was then, where do you spend most of your time?

It certainly wasn't with their family. It was at work, on the computer or out at functions. Although they said their family was what was most important, it was not where they were spending most of their time.

Now I understand that we have to work. I myself have two businesses so I understand that the bulk of our time is at work. However, the point is that when we are not at work, or when we are structuring our lives to support who and what is most important, we can have the time with our families all while creating successful and thriving businesses or careers.

What is disheartening though is that research has shown that our children are only getting an average of three minutes per week of meaningful conversation with their parents. Three minutes!!

[¹. Herr – All sources given in Bibliography section at the end of the book.]

Now there is something terribly, terribly wrong with that.

Families are not spending time together like they used to. They are rushing through life, from one activity to the next, not stopping to connect, to be together and truly listen to each other.

The Internet has become the household demon, stealing time from families daily when they are home.

A study from the Annenberg Center for the Digital Future at the University of Southern California found that families only spend 18 hours a week together and most of that time is in front of the television. [². Annenberg Center]

Five-year-old Facebook's active user base surged to more than 200 million active users by 2007. [³ MacKenzie]

Our children are becoming slaves to the world of Facebook, Twitter, Instagram and other social media sites. Their lives are no longer their own as they are at the mercy of what other children say and post about them.

They are the generation of children who go to bed at night worried about what people are saying about them and waking up to check first thing in the morning.

It's an awful way for our children to live. And yet, as parents we are not taking the reins enough to help them navigate that world. Why do I say that? Because we're not spending the time with them like we should.

What about bullying? Why has it become such an epidemic? Who is responsible for the way our children are treating each other?

Don't look to the schools. Look in the mirror.

I have seen firsthand how much our families are disconnected.

It's normal now to not spend time together at the dinner table talking for thirty minutes about our day.

It's normal to not spend time with your children as we tuck them in, asking them about their day and truly listening.

It's normal to rush from one day to the next without appreciating all that we have and the time we have with our loved ones.

We miss out on opportunities to teach our children about respect, love, empathy and kindness. We're too busy watching television programs riddled with violence and crime. We let our children have full control of what they watch, what websites they visit, and the people they call their friends.

Let's look at these sobering statistics:

- 160,000 children miss school every day due to the fear of attack or intimidation by other students [4 Center for the Prevention of School-Aged Violence]
- 90% of 4th through 8th graders report being victims of bullying [5 Bullying Statistics]
- Bullying statistics say revenge is the strongest motivation for school shootings [6 Cassada]

- Suicide remains among the leading causes of death of children under 14 [7 American Association of Suicidology]
- A new review of studies in 13 countries found signs of apparent connection between bullying, being bullied and suicide [8 Kim]
- Suicide rates among 10 to 14-year-olds have grown more than 50 percent over the last three decades [9 American Association of Suicidology]

So where are we as parents as this is all going on? Shall we be honest with ourselves?

We are focusing on the wrong stuff, stuff that is not as important as our children and their well-being.

Shall we talk about teen depression?

It was once thought that depression was something only adults suffered with but it has become apparent to psychiatrists that teen depression is real and it's on the rise.

- About 20 percent of teens will experience teen depression before they reach adulthood. [10 Costello]
- The percentage of girls who experienced major depressive episodes tripled between the ages of 12 and 15 (from 5.1 to 15.2 percent) [11 SAMHSA]
- Fewer than one-half of children with a diagnosable mental disorder receive mental health services in a given year. [12 US Dept of HHS]
- Children or teens experiencing depression may not show significant behavioral disturbances—that is, the depression may be taking an internal toll without disrupting the family—parents sometimes "hope for the best" or fail to get a child evaluated [13 NAMH]

- Studies show that there is a correlation between family meals and psychosocial well-being among adolescents [[14] Eisenberg] and yet slightly more than a quarter (28%) of adults with children under the age of 18 report that their families eat dinner together at home seven nights a week. [[15] Mason]

Our lives are extremely busy and studies are showing that our children's mental health is becoming directly related to the overburdened lives they face with social media, online access and overstuffed lives.

As parents, it is our role to provide for our children and we all want to do it to the best of our abilities. We want our children to have better lives than we had when we were growing up.

Long hours, working late into the evenings, texting, emailing, being online are all taking their toll on our families. We are becoming more and more disconnected from our children when we mean well and want to do our best as parents.

But the reality is – the stuff that we fill our lives with, the physical stuff like clothes, an expensive home, all the newest electronics and gadgets do not make our children happy. What they need most is undivided time with us, and that's become more and more scarce because of the choices we are making.

You are what they want. They want time with you. Fun times with you. Happy times with you. Joy-filled times with you.

But be honest and ask yourself where are you spending most of your time?

I have found more often than not that what we say is important and what we honor in our lives are two very different things.

And perhaps you had the glimpse of that realization with the walk-thru of your home or by reading the above statistics.
Either way, the goal is to get us all to start thinking of what is going on in our lives so that we can see how our stuff is creating the story that represents us and our lives. It's also about seeing how it's affecting everything else in our lives.

If we were to look at all areas of our lives, what would we see? What if we did a mental and physical walk-thru of our finances, of our relationships, of our health and well-being? What would it say to us?

These are tough questions because they force us to look at our lives through what the stuff is saying. It's not about what we think it is saying but it's about what it is reflecting back to us.

This stuff, the emotional, the financial and relationship stuff, is just as important, if not more important, than the physical stuff in our lives. The real important stuff is our health & well-being, our financial security, our relationships and our overall sense of joy and love for our lives.

That is the stuff that makes a life rich. Not the physical stuff that clutters our homes, offices and garages. That is just stuff to fill our lives not *fulfill* our lives.

That's the real truth.

That's the undeniable truth.

So before we close out this chapter, let's look at your stuff again.

The stuff in your home, your office, your garage.

The stuff in your attic, your basement, and your backyard shed.

The stuff in your kitchen cupboards and all the drawers.

The stuff in your closets, your vanities and in your cubby holes.

And let's also look at your finances, your relationships, your health and well-being, and your overall sense of joy and happiness.

Let's look at it all.

Where are you today? What is that stuff saying to you? What is it saying *about* you?

And remember, as you look at it, hold no judgment. It is nothing but an opportunity to make it different, make it better, from this point on.

And that's exactly what we are going to do – we're going to make it different. We're going to make it better.

We're going to look at the stories your stuff is saying and we're going to get to the heart of it and start downsizing your stuff so you can have around you what is truly important and special, in all areas of your life.

Imagine having in your life, in your home, only the things that bring you the greatest joy and make you feel absolutely wonderful? Imagine opening up the space in your life to have time for your children, your parents, for what is truly important for you?

It is possible and that is what we will do.

It's going to be an incredible and freeing experience, that I can promise you.

Letting go and moving forward keeping around you what is truly important and special will absolutely improve your life dramatically.

CHAPTER FOUR

Your Purge Will Set You Free

"Your life does not get better by chance, it gets better by change."
Jim Rohn

As I walked outside from the hospital room, on that warm May 30th, 2007 morning, exhausted, exasperated, feeling worn out, I prayed to God for a message of what I could learn that day.

I had been with Mom for more than six weeks. The task of caring for her, despite being in the hospital was taking a toll on me. I was tired due to the lack of restful sleep and waking several times during the night to ensure Mom was breathing.

I ached everywhere from sleeping on a cot that felt more like the lumpy, hard and uneven ground I slept on while camping in a tent many years ago.

I longed to be back home with my husband and kids whom I missed enormously.

I was tired. I was worn. I wanted a break. I wanted to go home.

The sun was shining and the warmth of its rays was a comfort from the coolness of the hospital room. The breeze blowing through my hair reminded me of my husband's tender fingers combing through my hair.

I wanted to go home.

As I walked to the park across from the hospital, I heard a quiet little voice from within me whisper *"stop waiting for"*.

Stop waiting for? Stop waiting for what?

"Stop waiting for her to die."

The shock of those words struck me. I knew that I had been doing just that. I had gotten so weary from caring for Mom that I forgot the real meaning for my being with her.

Sure it was the fatigue and I was feeling worn. But hearing those words snapped me back to what was important.

In that instant I realized how often I have thought of "when she dies….", "when I'm back home…", "when I'm with the Luc and the kids again…"

It made perfect sense to me especially since I knew my siblings and I, my husband and my children, we all had all begun to live "waiting for Mom to die so we could get back to our lives."

Meanwhile, there were probably many wonderful moments that we were letting slip by because we kept thinking, focusing on, what life would be like after we were done *waiting for*.

The more I thought about it, the more I didn't want to focus on *waiting for* any longer. I'd come back to my original intention of being with Mom, to ensure that every moment was special for her and that she would be my #1 focus again.

An overwhelming sense of love and gratitude came over me. I was happy. The fatigue that plagued me a few minutes earlier had dissipated and I was feeling fully rejuvenated.

Everything was as it was supposed to be and I was so thankful I could be with Mom.

I was grateful for Luc and the kids and all that they were doing to support my being with her. I was thankful for the love and support I had from my siblings and their families, and from Luc's family. There was so much to be thankful for that it re-energized me. I was ready for more!

Some of the most amazing experiences happen when we least expect them. We just have to be open to allow them to unfold; to release control over things; to let time breathe.

Mom was going through so much change that was beyond her control. Her body was shutting down and she was getting increasingly weaker. As a witness to her depleting health, I also found the beauty in taking that transition and making it something loving and legacy-building for her, and for myself.

What mattered most in those very precious weeks was what was truly important – love, kindness, compassion, being there for each other, focusing on what she could do and letting go of what she couldn't do.

It was never about money, cars, houses or any other of stuff. It was about love. It was about connection. It was about her legacy in my life as she let go to move forward herself.

It was one of the best experiences of my life and I can assure you that the doctors and nurses were astounded by her amazing journey through end-of-life. We never focused on what she couldn't do. We focused on what she could do.

So when I talk about letting go and simplifying your life, what I am talking about is looking at where you are in your life so that you can determine what is truly important, what matters most and surround yourself with that. To keep in your world what nourishes you, makes you happy and brings you the greatest joy.

My experience has taught me that many of us are living lives that feel empty and yet our homes are overstuffed. Our lives are overstuffed. We feel like we are longing for more and yet the stuff we do have isn't enough.

We're also living lives of *waiting for*. We're waiting for the weekend, or the vacation or time off. We're waiting to lose weight, or start another diet or buy the gym membership. We're waiting to make more money, or change jobs, or get a raise. We're *waiting for*.

That *waiting for* affects our letting go. It keeps up us stuck, stuck in our stuff.

You can look around your home and see that much of what you have has been *waiting for*…your time, money, to lose weight, for the kids to leave, or the kids to come home, for your partner to love you. Or for you to love yourself.

You've been *waiting for*.

It's time to stop *waiting for*. It's time to take control of your life, focus on what is important to you and let go so you can have what you value most.

We've done part of this in the previous chapter but you really have to get real here before we can even begin to move forward. This is no time to play. This is the time to get really serious about what matters most to you and what you want the most.

And may I just say that what you want may not be what you need.

You may need to stop spending and take fiscal responsibility for you and your family.

You may need therapy or counseling to reconcile some serious pain you have experienced.

You may need to join a weight loss program that will get you back to feeling healthy.

It's no longer time to *wait for*. It's time to make a decision and take action!

Right now, I want you to determine what you want. The Big Why of your today and your tomorrows. What do you want for your health, your relationships, for your finances, for your work and for your overall joy and happiness? What do you really, really want?

In my program "Your Abundant Life: 5 Fast Ways to Creating the Life You Want With Less", we walk through a process of determining what it is you really want. It's a powerful yet simple exercise that I'd like to share with you.

The first step is to decide what you do like about your life and what you do not like.

When we work with clients and we're meeting for the first time during the consultation, the purpose is to find out what it is they are most challenged with and what are their strengths. We assess where they are and ask questions to discover where they'd like to be after working with us.

When you are creating your life vision, it is the same thing. You'll need to look at where you are today, in all areas of your life, and compare it to what it is you truly want, based on what is important in your life.

Sandy was a stay-at-home mother. She had a very busy schedule taking care of her three children. Her home had become a hub of activity for her young family and each room showed it.

There were toys and clothes strewn on the floor in almost every room. Bookcases were stuffed with books while toy boxes overflowed.

She wanted desperately to clean up her home, organize it so that she could gain a sense of peace and her children could learn about responsibility and teamwork.

Our main objective when we first met with her was to determine where she was struggling the most, what caused her the most amount of stress and dissatisfaction and determine what she was great at doing on her own and where she would need the most help.

It wasn't long that through the clutter of her home, we found the clutter in other areas of her life. They were stretched financially even though they purchased the best toys and latest electronics for their children.

Sandy couldn't shed the weight because her priorities were her children and being a mother.

She wanted more time with her spouse to rekindle the romance but she was always so tired and worn out from her day.

For her, to have a system, a plan, a way to keep her home organized and tidy would allow her the emotional space to focus on other areas of her life that were just as cluttered as her home.

Working with her, the children and her spouse was a very rewarding experience for them all. They were able to look at where they were and determine what they really wanted, based on what was truly important.

> *They were able to create a vision for their home that had them all focused and working together. They sorted and purged what they no longer needed, used or wanted and only kept what they knew they would use and enjoy.*
>
> *This process was cathartic for the other areas of their lives. They were able to take the vision for their home and match it to what they wanted financially, what they wanted for their health and well-being and what they wanted for their relationships.*
>
> *By looking at their physical world, they were able to create a vision for their entire lives.*

I love the process of what a vision creates. It truly engages the entire person to look at all areas of their lives to determine what they like now, what is missing and what they truly want.

It's not just about the stuff. And it's no longer about *waiting for*. It's about paying attention to everything in your life and asking yourself what you want each area to look like, just like what we did with Sandy and her home.

So here's your chance – a chance to start a new chapter in your life by looking at where you are and determine what you really, really want.

In the following exercise, take a few minutes to ask yourself what is missing from each area and determine what it is you really want. Be honest with yourself and don't let a "dream too big" bog you down. If you want to be a wealthy, and you absolutely feel it is extremely important and a priority, then write it down. If you are saying to yourself that you really want to get out of debt, be specific and write down the amount you will need to be clear of your debt. Don't worry about the "how" at this point. This exercise if for you to get clear on where you are and what you want.

When I work privately with clients, we work on a concise timeline that meets their most important goals. It can be based on a 90-day action plan or a one-year plan, but all are based on a longer-term vision of what they truly want for their lives – in all areas of their lives.

When I am working with a family or an individual in a home transition that plan is based on timelines and deadlines imposed by the sale of the property or the closing date on their home.

Either way, we are working on a concise timeline and I recommend the same here.

For this exercise, I'd like you to focus on a short-term plan, three or six months. You can do this same exercise for a one-year, two-year, or five-year plan later if you like. For now, let's focus on a shorter-term timeline so you can get to experience quick and gratifying results.

So let's get started. Write down <u>one to three</u> things you want for each area of your life within the next three to six months. Be very specific and quantify your goals with numbers. Go!

HEALTH & WELL-BEING

_____

_____

_____

_____

FINANCES

_____
_____
_____
_____

RELATIONSHIPS

_____
_____
_____
_____

FAMILY

_____
_____
_____
_____

FUN & ADVENTURE

_____
_____
_____
_____

SPIRITUALLY

_____
_____
_____
_____

COMMUNITY

_____
_____
_____
_____

YOUR HOME

_____
_____
_____
_____

The clearer you get, and the more specific you are, the easier the next steps will be. So get really, really clear.

I'd be willing to bet that your goals and objectives are based on the following: more energy, lose weight, more money, more time with family, more time to do the things that you love, new experiences, more adventures, more connected to your purpose and your life's meaning.

Those are all great things to want and they are very universal.

Most people want to be healthier, live happier, have better relationships, deeper meaning in their lives and have financial freedom.

The truth is not everyone is willing to commit to doing what it takes to make that happen.

It's one thing to want it. It's another thing to make it a priority and do what you have to make it happen.

So I'm going to give you a step-by-step approach that works like a charm with my clients. It's not a standard way of setting goals. It's not a standard way of looking at our lives.

But having been through a lot of stuff with my clients, I can assure you, this process is one that is liberating and works.

And the first step is to start with a sort and a purge.

Yup! That's what I said. A sort and a purge.

In the exercise above, you looked at what you wanted in your life. I asked you to assess what is missing and determine what it is you really want.

Great!

Now we're going to get rid of stuff. Why? So you can make room for the stuff that you really, really want. The stuff that you said was most important.

We're going to stop *waiting for*. Instead we are going to be *striving for*.

I know that the mere sound of the word "purge" makes people cringe. No one wants to give up stuff they love, want to keep or just feel they may need one day.

But without the purge, you will remain bogged down and stuck exactly where you are, in the stuff that is no longer serving you or helping you to move forward.

Before we get to the purge though, I'd like to share this story with you.

> *Meet Elizabeth. She's an amazing woman who has what would appear to be a thriving business coaching practice. When we first met, she told me she wanted to bring her business to the next level but she found herself stuck. It wasn't as though she wasn't working her business but there was something that was keeping her from making the move to the next level.*
>
> *During our time together, we looked at her practice and saw that there were clients that she had outgrown. She had really upleveled her skills and a few of her clients were no longer the right fit for her practice.*
>
> *Ironically, when we looked at her bedroom closet, we found a similar situation. There were clothes that no longer fit her and that she no longer wanted to wear.*

> *She also had taken the time several months ago to start downsizing her closet and had bagged several trash bags of clothes that she had intended to bring to charity, but took up space in her basement.*
>
> *To me, it was obvious. She was stuck because she was not letting go of what no longer served her or fit her. She was also holding on to things she had tried to let go.*
>
> *Purging her closet helped her to purge her client list. By letting go of what was no longer a good fit for her, she was able to create the space to breathe, and feel a sense of peace. She also opened up herself, her closet and her practice to what was truly a good fit and would help her uplevel her life.*

We all have stuff that is keeping us stuck and that no longer fits us. When we are feeling bogged down, it's not because we are not trying to move forward. There's just no room for the good stuff to come in. We're not letting go first in order to move forward.

So I want you to start looking at your stuff, ALL OF YOUR STUFF, from this point on by asking yourself if it is holding you back, moving you forward, hurting you or keeping you stuck.

Is it still a good fit?

Do you absolutely love it?

Is it time to let it go?

That's it.

Every 'thing' in your life, and I mean every *thing*, is a metaphor for what is going on in your life.

And the fastest way to improve your life is to sort and purge.

Your purge will set you free!

Remember the walk-thru we did in the third chapter? Take a look at your notes and let's look at it again but this time with the unscrupulous eyes of the Sort & Purge.

In all seriousness, nothing will change until you decide what is truly important in your life by looking at how your stuff is helping you or hindering you.

So how do you start the Sort & Purge? Let's get to it!

CHAPTER FIVE

Letting Go to Move Forward

*"Holding on is believing that there's only a past;
letting go is knowing that there's a future."
Daphne Rose Kingma*

"It was really great to meet you", I say as I hug her so tightly.

We are standing in the family room on the third floor of the hospital, by the nurses' station and just a few steps from our mothers' rooms. Night after night, she and I would get together for a few minutes to share stories, comfort each other and just be with each other. We understood one another and what we were going through.

Our mothers were dying.

On this particular night, we were facing the stark reality that this could be our last night together. Her mother's condition had taken a turn for the worse and they were preparing for her passing.

The television in the family room became our greatest ally. For the past few weeks, the hockey playoffs were on and we'd meet for thirty minutes in the evenings to catch a glimpse of what the outside world was experiencing.

It connected us through our love of sports and it grounded us in the knowing that there was life outside of our mother's hospital rooms.

Back home, our Ottawa Senators were in the finals against the Pittsburg Penguins. It was the first game of the best of seven series and the Sens had just won the game.

We had celebrated their victory and were immediately brought back to the reality that her mother may die before mine, and she'd be the first to go back to her life.

During my time with her, I appreciated her friendship and her support. Most importantly, I appreciated her presence and her understanding of what I was going through.

Tonight, we were letting go. Noralee was preparing to say good-bye to her mother and I was letting go of the friend that had comforted me for so many nights. I knew that my turn to let go of my mother was fast approaching and saying good bye to her was just a first of many more letting go's I'd have to go through.

Letting go is not an easy process. Had I only known back then how much I'd have to shed through the process of losing my mother. Truth is, it hasn't ended. I continue to shed and trust I will continue to do so for the rest of my life.

Following my mother's death, I immersed myself in the study of death and dying, bereavement and grief recovery. I loved learning about what I was going through and how I could potentially help others later in my journey.

In all of my bereavement studies, what I've discovered is that part of the physical letting go in helping someone move through loss is the emotional letting go that is at the core of it all.

Through time and process, space is given to the grieving person to experience the feelings of loss all while helping them take steps to move forward into a new phase of their lives with the object or person they are grieving no longer present. Releasing the emotional attachment they have to the physical person or object is the key to moving forward.

Dr. John Bowlby and Mary Ainsworth developed the *Attachment Theory* [[16] Bretherton] after studying mothers and their children for more than thirty years. Through their findings, they determined that our attachment is based on feeling a sense of security and safety that supports our very survival.

> *Roger came to us three years after his wife had passed away. He had met another woman and they were planning on moving into a new home together. That meant downsizing his belongings and selling his current home, the home in which he had lived for more than twenty-five years raising his children with his late wife.*
>
> *When I first met him, I knew he was very much grieving the loss of his wife and the life he had with her. Although he was starting a new chapter with another woman whom he loved, he was stuck in the past, struggling to let go to move forward.*
>
> *For more than six months we worked with him, starting in areas that were far easier to tackle: closets with his clothes, the kitchen cupboards and his adult daughters' bedrooms.*
>
> *By working in areas that held little emotional charge for him, we were able to get him working his purge muscle. Day after day, he worked diligently at sorting through what he no longer needed, used or wanted.*

> *What we saved for last was his office and family room filled with books. The rooms were literally wall-to-wall bookcases of books and the books meant so much to Roger.*
>
> *Many of the books were for research when he published his first book many years ago. He was very much attached to the time he spent studying, writing and eventually publishing his book.*
>
> *The remaining books were those of his children and his late wife and they all held a very personal connection to him.*
>
> *To us, they were books.*
>
> *To him, they represented memories and a past filled with love, connection and happiness.*
>
> *It was extremely difficult and emotionally challenging for him to downsize the number of books to only keep the ones that meant the most to him.*
>
> *It was a process, which took time, patience and a gentleness afforded to those who are trapped in the past.*
>
> *He got through it and the transformation he experienced was incredible. Roger is not the same man we met several months ago. He has moved into his new home and is creating new memories with the woman he loves.*
>
> *Through the process of letting go, Roger is now moving forward.*

Roger's experience may resonate with you or someone that you know. Letting go of our stuff and the memory it has to the person that we love is not an easy process. It takes time and it takes a sense of gentleness to get through it all.

Note that we are never asking you or a client to let go of the person you love or the memories that you have. We are strictly looking at the physical objects that are part of what is keeping you from moving forward. We want you to be able to move through the letting go of the physical objects to keep your memories and the bond that you have with the person you love intact. It's vitally important. The goal is to let go of the object, not the memory or the person that you love.

As for Roger (and for you) starting in an area that was easier for him afforded him the opportunity to get used to letting things go, to move through the process with greater ease.

Once we got to the harder, more emotional parts of his transition, he had gained a strength he didn't have when we first started working with him. That strength got him to look at his books with a new perspective. He was building a new life, he was moving forward and it was time to let go of what didn't fit in his new life.

I'm happy to report that Roger is doing well and he is enjoying his new life, his new home and the person he has become following his life transition.

So now it's your turn. It's time to start looking at what you said you wanted in the previous chapter and align that with what is currently in your life and begin the Sort & Purge!

Let's start with a physical space. You're going to want to keep in mind the vision you have for your life. The goal you set for each of the areas of your life will be your compass. As you begin to sort and purge each space in your home, you're going to remind yourself what you said you wanted, what was most important to you, and that will guide you in this process.

To begin, you're going to want to do what we recommend to all clients - start with an area or a space that is easiest. Avoid starting with an area that is overwhelming or emotionally charged.

Instead, start with an area or a space that holds little to no emotional attachment. A linen closet is a great place to start!

As you begin to go through your physical stuff, start noticing the subtle messages you are receiving from going through it all.

Are you feeling happy to let it go?

Are you wondering why you kept it for so long?

Are you upset you didn't sort and purge sooner?

The process of letting go of your physical stuff will bring with it the emotional, psychological and perhaps the spiritual stuff too.

Are you finding by letting go of this stuff, you are getting closer to your goals, to the vision of what you want?

You'll be amazed by how wonderful you'll feel when you've tackled a space or two that was easy to get through and how it begins to bring you closer to your goals. Hold onto that feeling, you'll need it later!

The process of going through your physical stuff also requires you to use a system so that what you are purging doesn't stay in your home. It needs to be removed and the sooner, the better.

The process we use is quite simple. You have only four choices when you hold up an item.

1. Keep
2. Donate/Gift
3. Recycle
4. Trash

That's it. It really is that simple. Don't try to overcomplicate things. This will stop you in your tracks and you'll see no progress.

Follow our system and you'll be pleasantly surprised by how much you can get through, purge and remove from your home.

What happens when you do get stuck on an item and you're not sure what would be best?

Go back to your vision of what you want for that space, that room, your life. That is where you will find the answer.

When we're talking about your physical stuff, you need to look at every single piece that you own and ask yourself how important it is in your life right now, today, and how it will help you or hinder you moving forward.

This is not a time to say that you may use it someday so you should keep it especially when you have not used it, worn it or even thought of it for over 6 months to a year. That is a serious statement. What are you doing keeping something that you haven't even thought of for all of this time?

Remember, we are no longer *waiting for*. Let it go.

The other thing I'd like you to do is work in small blocks of time.

When we work with clients, we do not spend full days sorting and purging, unless we are working on a very tight deadline or we're working with families who live out-of-town and have come in to help.

The task of sorting and purging is physically and emotionally exhausting. We are very mindful of the state of being of each client and focusing on the process in small blocks of time allows them to stay focused on what is important to complete on that day without getting to the point of exhaustion or feeling overwhelmed.

As a good rule of thumb, a 3-4 hour block of time works well. It's not too long and it's not too short.

It's also enough time to help the person make mental and emotional adjustments along the way on his or her own. As they are going through their items, making decisions about what to keep, gift, donate or throw away, they are re-evaluating what is really important in their lives. They are making small choices for big results.

Anyone can do this at home by sorting through a closet, a basement, or a garage. Having a vision of what is really important and then experiencing the sorting process from that perspective makes the task a lot easier.

Deciding what to keep becomes a matter of how it will serve the vision of your life. If something no longer fits, is out of style or hasn't been worn for more than a year, letting it go to charity is far easier when you know it's no longer for the person you are now or moving forward to being.

Continue to use this process one space at a time, one room at a time until you've reached the vision you wanted. It will take time, it will take discipline and commitment but the end result will be everything you wanted it to be – a transformation.

When you're dealing with other areas of your life, you will follow the same process.

You will acknowledge where you are and where you want to be based on what is truly important. That vision will then empower you to make the decisions you need to make to let go of what is no longer serving you and keep what is of most importance and value.

When you are focusing on your health, and you are starting to look at what you need to sort and purge, you can start in your kitchen.

The kitchen is ultimately the first place to start. What do you have in your kitchen that is hurting you rather than helping you?

I don't have to go into detail here. You know what is healthy and what is not and if you are not sure, the rule of thumb is to eat foods in their most natural state. If they are processed in any way, you are putting into your body what is not the best or most important for you. Eat what is fresh, in its most natural state and avoid foods that have no nutritional value.

The next place to sort and purge, when it comes to your health and well-being, is your schedule. You *HAVE* to make the time to move your body. We were not born to live sedentary lives. Look back at your childhood. How much time did you spend at home doing nothing? Not much. You were outside running, playing hide-and-go-seek, or going on adventures on your bicycle with friends.

Today as we know this is a far different story and has led to an overweight and obese society.

In February 2012, the Institute of Medicine (IOM) released a study that showed that nearly 69 percent of U.S. adults (2 in 3) and 32 percent of children (1 in 3) are either overweight or obese. [[17] Institute of Medicine]

This is a sobering statistic and one that is extremely alarming especially when being overweight or obese has been proven to lead to many health problems that can be irreversible. It's also a very uncomfortable way to live.

So let's go back to your vision. This is about you. What are you doing to be physically active and healthy every day?

If you are saying you do not have the time to exercise and take care of yourself, well, guess what? That won't cut it. That just means you are putting everything else ahead of your own health and well-being.

Working with seniors affords me a crystal-ball opportunity to see into the future. Many of them share with us their regret to have not taken better care of themselves when they were younger and had the chance to make changes.

They'd give anything to go back and live healthier and more active lives. They all thought that they'd be well in their later years but the truth is what they did in their past has led to the many hardships and challenges they are now facing.

Their message to me and my young team - don't waste your health on things that are not important and make your health and well-being a priority.

As for your relationships, you'll want to look at how much time and effort you are putting into making your relationships strong, loving and important in your life.

I recently saw Bishop T.D. Jakes give a sermon about commitment and relationships and what stood out for me was something I strongly believe in. [18 Jakes]

He said that we had to be there for our loved ones. We had to show up for them. We made a commitment when we had children that we'd be there for them no matter what and that we'd do the same for our spouses when we married. He also said that as parents, when we give so much to our children, we want them to be there for us when we are older and need their help.
What is happening though is that we are not showing up for our aging parents. We are not spending enough time with our children. We are not putting in the effort to be the best partner to our spouses.

Everything else is more important and our relationships are suffering.

The truth is, there is no greater blessing in our lives than our loved ones. When you honor your family, you honor your best self.

In his book *The Four Things That Matter Most: A Book About Living* [19 Byock], Dr. Ira Byock, an international leader in palliative care, demonstrates through the stories of his patients and their families that our most valuable possessions are the relationships with those we love. When a family member is facing death, material possessions do not matter. What matters most is the time left with our loved ones, saying what needs to be said, creating lasting and loving memories all while honoring the depth of the relationship.

It's not about stuff.

I understand that family dynamics can be challenging and that some family members can push every single hot button we have. But in all truth, what really matters when all is said and done is family and friends and the love that we share.

Many people will hide behind the busyness of their lives and not show up for their family. They often realize how late it is when that family member has died.

I'm sure you have heard of this happening or maybe you have experienced it for yourself.

Losing someone as important as a family member or a friend after not having them be an integral and important part of your life is almost always devastating and hard to recover from.

Family is what we are born into and love is what we leave behind. The space between is up to us to make as rich and as special as possible.

I understand that there are times when you have to walk away from someone because their values and their way of life do not fit with yours. What I'm really talking about is making the time and the commitment to be there for those that are there for you and for those that mean the most to you.

It really is that simple.

It may require having to say no to other things or saying 'not now'. Only you can determine what is most important to you and that is your compass. Use your vision and what is truly important to determine how you will sort and purge your schedule and create the time you want for what is most important.

In all areas of your life, this will be the same process. In your health, finances, relationships and overall sense of joy and happiness, you'll have to look at the overall picture of things and start sorting and purging.

There will be areas that will be easier to sort through, to purge and decide upon, while others will overwhelm you, have you feeling stuck and unable to get through it.

Your guiding force will be your plan, your vision and knowing what is really important to you. That is how you will make a decision about everything in your life – from the food that you eat, to the friends that you keep, to the movies that you watch – everything that you decide to keep in your life has to be important, honored and empowering you in a very positive way. If not, it's time to let it go.

And you can do it. I know you can. Why? Because you got this far in the book. Congratulations!!

I would bet that most people who purchased this book didn't get past the first chapter because they were not committed to making a significant and lasting change in their lives.

But you did it! And that means a whole lot. It means so much!! And you my friend will reap the rewards. You got this far. You can go the rest of the way!

Those that truly commit to making a change and improving their lives have the greatest results. They are the ones that live in a place of least regret and most joy and satisfaction. I trust that is where you want to be as well.

Their lives are abundant because they keep only what is most special, what is most important and what is most valuable in their lives.

They honor their relationships.

They honor their health and well-being.

They honor their finances.

They honor their lives.

Making major changes in one's life is huge. It's HUGE! Most people want to improve their lives, they talk about it, but they never commit and take the action to do it, to go the entire way.

You, on the other hand, are different. You want this and you're willing to do what it takes to make it happen.

You don't want to live paycheck to paycheck anymore.

You don't want to be bogged down by stuff you don't need, use or want.

You want happier and stronger relationships with your loved ones.

You want to make a noticeable and lasting difference in the lives of others.

You want to leave behind a legacy that will inspire.

And you're doing what you have to to make it all happen.

You will see and feel the incredible transformation that comes from sorting, purging and living an abundant life that is filled with what you love most.

And to celebrate, please don't go buy more 'stuff'! Please commemorate your milestones by honoring what you are going through with family and friends through sharing, love and being together.

No need to have a large spread of food.

No need to consume an excess amount of alcohol.

No need to go on a shopping spree.

It's about honoring the commitment you had to yourself, your loved ones and what is truly important to you through a celebration the old fashioned way – being together, talking, honoring and celebrating with love.

Noralee is a part of my story. She helped me so much through my journey with my mother and we honored each other by being there for each other each night. She will continue to be part of the story of my life and I'm grateful she was part of my letting go journey.

Create your story, your memory book that you will one day leave behind. Live your life to the absolute fullest now, honoring the people and the stuff that is most important to you.

This is the recipe to an abundant life.

It's your stuff. It's your story. It's your life.

Let's continue!

CHAPTER SIX

A Second Chance to Let Go

"My favorite fruit is grapes, because with grapes, you always get another chance. 'Cause, you know, if you have a crappy apple or a peach, you're stuck with that crappy piece of fruit. But if you have a crappy grape, no problem - just move on to the next. 'Grapes: The Fruit of Hope.'"
Demetri Martin

"Look up!" I hear from that internal voice. *"Look up!"* I hear with a sense of urgency.

I'm sitting in my backyard, dazed and lost. Mom had her stroke two days ago and I've been calling the hospital every two hours to check on her and I've been waiting, cell phone in hand for "the" call.

I'm a wreck. I want so much to go back home and be with Mom but I'm being told there's nothing I can do. So I wait, in agony, minute by minute, as time drags on.

"Look up!" I hear again.

As I lift my weary head and try to focus on the sky, I see a puff of clouds that is most definitely shaped like an angel. I'm stunned but know well enough to call my husband and daughter who are near me to look up.

"Briana! Luc!" I shout. "Look up! Look up! Do you see what I see? Do you see her?"

As they come running over, and look up at the sky, they simultaneously and rhythmically say "An angel!"

"Mom! Mom!" I say out loud. My heart is racing and I'm shaking. It's a sign!

I run into the house to grab the camera.

"I have to capture the picture! I have to capture Mom's angel!"

I rush to my office, my eyes are blurred with excitement. "Where is the camera?"

I'm looking madly through the junk in my office. "Where is the camera? Oh God, please let me find the camera!"

"There it is!" I grab the camera, fumble with it to find the on switch and run outside.

"Is she still there?" I ask desperately.

"Yes!" my husband and daughter sing in unison.

I raise the camera and focus on the most beautiful angel I have ever seen. I press the button and she is captured forever.

As I realize the magnitude of this blessing, I sit down next to my daughter and cry.

"Oh Mom!" I cry. "Oh Mom!"

"It's a sign from God", my daughter says, comforting me. "She's going to go to Heaven and they are coming for her."

I hold onto my daughter and weep tears of joy.

"Thank you for the sign", I whisper. "Thank you for letting me know she's going to be ok."

The angel I saw on that day was a powerful reminder to be in the moment and appreciate all that I had and all that I experienced with Mom. It was also a sign that I was to let go and allow time to unfold as it was meant to be.

It wouldn't be until many years later that the angel and her significance would be a sign to let go and move forward. It wouldn't be until many anniversaries of her passing that I would understand that letting go was a beautiful part of the experiences we have in life.

Letting go frees us. It opens up possibility. It brings in riches we could never have expected.

So let's look at that now, again. Let's look at letting go from a perspective of richness and possibility.

We've talked about looking at where you are in your life and creating a vision for what you truly want based on what is most important.

You've done a walk-thru of your home and every area of your life. You've set one goal to achieve within the next 3-6 months for each of those areas. And you've set the Sort & Purge in motion.

And yet, you may be feeling like you're not moving forward fast enough. You may be feeling an emotional overwhelm just at the thought of letting go of your stuff.

When you are working through the letting go process on your own, you are likely to get stuck, feel overwhelmed and stop the process entirely.

So we're going to look at the letting go process again but this time, we're going to approach it from the perspective of opportunity and grace.
Let me assure you that purging is not an easy process. It's about letting go and letting go is not easy for most of us because we're so used to hanging on to everything, regardless of if it's good for us or not.

We want to hold on to things that once meant something to us because we're afraid of what it will be like once we let it go. And yet, I'd like to assure you that the letting go process, despite it being a difficult one, is extremely rewarding in so many ways.

When you pick up an item and you look at it, when you feel it, you immediately have a visceral reaction to it. Your body reacts to it and you are immediately taken back to the time the item meant something to you.

I like to use the metaphor of a movie playing in your mind. In the movie, there are people and characters; there is a scene and a storyline. The moment you pick up the item, the movie starts to play.

You are now part of the movie. It may be happy, joyous and fun, or it may be heartbreaking, poignant or sad. In the movie, you are immediately taken back to the place and the time when that item had its greatest meaning.

The movie stirs up all the emotions that the storyline depicts. You can feel the same emotions as though you were back in time, with that item, as the movie unfolds in your mind.

It has a strong representation to you and you want so much to hold onto the item, to the memory, especially if it represents someone you love, a time of great happiness, or something of great importance.

It's the memory that keeps you from letting go.

Although your mind can rationally say "let go", your heart says "hold on".

When I work with clients, I don't know the story behind an item. To me, it is what it is. There's no history, no feelings attached to it. It's an item. For the individual or the family however, it is much more than that. It's a moment in time, a connection to someone they love, a memory to hold onto.

When the item has little significant value to a client, it's an easy process. The client can simply say, "I don't need this. It means nothing. I can let it go."

However when the item means far more than it simply being what it is, the person can then get stuck in the memory and freeze.

Perhaps this has happened to you in your purge. Perhaps you came across an item that brought you back to a time of great love and joy or a time of loss and sadness. Perhaps you found yourself reliving a time in your past that you wanted to enjoy again or perhaps you found yourself longing to be in that moment again.

The item and the meaning it holds is precious. You don't want to let it go.

And it's that desire that keeps us from moving forward. It can keep us stuck, and stuck for a very long time.

Do you remember Roger's story? He was stuck in the memory of living with his wife and raising his children in their family home. Despite knowing it was time to move forward, sell the house and start a new chapter in his life, he found himself overwhelmed with emotion and a flood of memories every time we sorted a room or an area that brought back deep and profound memories. His movie reel was playing and he was fully engaged in the show.

It wasn't until he could watch the movie and embrace his memories rather than want to relive them did he begin to make the decisions that ultimately got him to move forward. Once he got to a place of reconciliation with where he was now could he look at his old items and begin the process of letting go.

And letting go he did. Although the memory-movie still played in his mind and it tugged at his heart, he stayed in the present and foresaw his future with his new partner. He let go of the items and moved forward.

We honored his late wife, their children and the memories that their items and the house held. We encouraged him to keep a special place for the memories of he and his late wife and children. He'll always have those and what is most special to him in his heart. What he let go of as physical stuff has freed him to create new memories and move forward.

Another reason people struggle with letting go is when they feel a deep need to stay in control of everything. One way to stay in control is to hold onto things. If you were to tell someone that you were taking something away because they didn't need it anymore, they would most likely fight you and tell you that they do, even when they know deep down you are right.

Rather than let something go, they will hold onto it because they are afraid of losing control.

Hey! I get it. I like to be in control of things too. I want to know what's going on and when. I like to make my own decisions and don't like when they are made for me.

As we get older, and we start feeling like things are not always within our control, I often see people holding onto things when they should be letting them go simply to stay in control.

> *Remember Eddy, our family friend. He had lost a lot within a short amount of time. He lost his wife, his mobility, and his independence. He was forced to leave his apartment and be at the mercy of what others could do for him.*
>
> *He was no longer in control of many things in his life.*
>
> *When we moved him into our home, we packed much of what he had in boxes and some bags. What is important to share here is that he had five garbage bags of linens and towels that he no longer used but wanted us to move.*
>
> *They sat in my basement for the five months he was here, untouched. I had encouraged him to sort through them the week before he moved into his new apartment but they remained untouched.*
>
> *On move day, he requested that the bags be moved to his new apartment.*

> *Despite knowing that he would not use any of the contents, we moved the bags.*
>
> *The bags still sit in his bedroom closet in his new apartment.*

Despite us knowing that what was in the garbage bags would no longer serve him in his new home, he felt compelled to keep them as a way of staying in control. We could have easily taken the items and donated them to charity on his behalf. However, the mere thought of taking the bags away made him feel anxious and upset. He needed to keep the bags of stuff. He needed to stay in control.

If you are feeling this way, you should ask yourself what you are afraid to lose. Are you afraid that by letting go you're letting go of control?

Losing control is a great fear for many, especially as we age. We want to stay in control of what is going on in our lives and ultimately we want to make the decisions about how things unfold. That also means making the decisions as to what we keep, what we don't and what we want in our lives.

It will come down to your priorities and what is most important in your life. Knowing what is at the top of the list will certainly help you determine where things fit in the hierarchy of what you need to hold onto and keep. And this pertains to all areas of your life.

Another reason people struggle and get stuck in their stuff is because of the value or sense of importance or worth they put on something.

We often see families valuing items that have long lost their monetary value. We are told that their items should be worth more than what they are presently in the market. However, it's a fact that items lose their value especially when the market is flooded with them.

> *Anthony and his brother were left with the task to empty and sell their parents' home when their mother moved into a retirement home. Because their mother had dementia, she could no longer make decisions and Anthony was entrusted to care for her items as her Power of Attorney.*
>
> *His mother had left several collections of china, Royal Doulton figurines and silverware. Anthony and his brother assumed they would bring in a sizeable amount once sold. However the reality was that with many other older adults downsizing and selling their property, the market was now being flooded with items of similar nature and value.*
>
> *Their uniqueness was a thing of the past as was their high value.*
>
> *On their behalf, the items were sold at auction and they were left feeling disappointed by the amount the items fetched. The appraiser however felt they received more than they would have gotten had they tried to sell them privately.*

It's a reality of our current world. Items are no longer worth what they were before and you should be prepared to face that fact if and when you plan on selling items you feel have great value.

When we place an unrealistic value on something it is likely to keep us stuck as we feel we need to receive what we feel it is worth, despite what the market says it is now worth.

It's tough when you think your great grandmother's china should be worth thousands when in fact it is only worth a few hundred dollars at best. Television programs like Pawn Stars and the Antique Roadshow have given the false impression that items could be worth thousands of dollars when in fact they are worth little today.

Doing research and asking professionals to establish the current value of your prized possessions is the surest way to protect yourself and help you make an informed decision. By knowing the value of an item, you are able to make a choice on what to do with it.

This holds true for other things in your life too. You may think that a friendship holds value because of the loyalty you owe it; however, if that person is no longer a positive and supportive energy in your life, it may be time to let them go so you can focus on those that are there to love and support you.
Look at all areas of your life and ask yourself if you are putting too much value on something or someone that is no longer serving you and helping you in your life.

What opportunities are you missing by holding on? What richness are you repelling because you are focused on what you will miss rather than what you will gain?

To facilitate this process look at your priorities, at what is truly important. We did this exercise in an earlier chapter and you should have a very good idea what is most important to you in every area of your life.

If something or someone is impeding your growth, your happiness or your health, it may be time to take a serious look at where they fit in your life. You really do not have to keep something or someone in your life because you feel that you have to.

This can get a little sticky when we talk about family. However, there are ways to ensure you remain civil and kind with family, stay connected to them, without them being an integral part of your day-to-day life. There are ways to ensure that they do not poison your world.

In case you need assistance with this, you can visit a bookstore, a library or search the topic online. There are countless books and resources available to you to help you navigate the world of family and your commitment to them. There is no need to be rude, hurtful or disrespectful. You can continue to build your life the way you want it to be, following your priorities and what is most important to you, without hurting others in the process. That is key – without hurting others in the process.

Feeling stuck in the process of letting go is often a normal and natural way of experiencing change. The problem lies in staying stuck.
The true joy of transition comes when you do let go, when you do take a step or two, or three to move forward. It doesn't have to happen all at once or overnight. It can take days, weeks and sometimes months.

The key is to take the steps, to continually do something to move forward towards what you want, to what you really, really want.

Stop focusing on what you will miss out on and focus on the opportunity of what you will gain.

Don't let yourself get stuck in the memories, nor in the fear of losing control. Take your time with it and let yourself see that the item is not the memory and that you are in control, even through this transition.

And when you find yourself thinking that something is worth more than it probably is, ask a professional's opinion. Often times, what you believe something is worth is not the value at all. Let yourself be freed by letting go of something that holds little or no value.

I'd like you to remember that you are moving forward and you are taking steps to create the life that you want. You are taking steps to look at your stuff so that you can lead a fully abundant life.

It is a process. It is a journey. It is rich in experience and rich in emotions. Enjoy the moments, each one of them, as you move through it all.

I was so blessed to receive that angel that day. She was a comfort then and she is a comfort now. Let go and honor the people, the loved ones, the experiences of your life. You are blessed every day with what is part of your life.

Take the time to really know what is important, be there for what and who is really important and keep your priorities in check. Great stuff is coming your way!

CHAPTER SEVEN

Legacy Matters

"A year from now you will wish you had started today."
Karen Lamb

I'm twenty-eight thousand feet above ground, in a thirty-two passenger Dash-8 airplane. It's noisy, the overhead compartments are rattling fiercely and I'm on my way to see my mother who is dying.

I'm feeling rushed to get to her. I'm desperate to get to her.

"Will I make it in time?" I think as I look at my watch, like the dials on the face of it have anything to do with her fate. "Will she die before I get to her?"

The thought of my children then comes to mind. I've been so busy. So terribly busy with work, growing two businesses. I'm afraid that I'm losing them. We're not as close as we used to be or should I say I don't spend as much time with them like I should.

I wonder if the busyness of my life and my self-imposed self-importance has created a riff between us like I have with my mother. I wonder about my legacy, the legacy that I am leaving behind with my children, and the memories for which they will remember me. Have I done enough? Am I a good mother?

Those thoughts fill my mind as they fight with the thoughts of my dying mother. As the reality of what is going on becomes ever so clear, I wonder how I measure up as a mother to my children.

~~~~~~~~~~~~~~~~~~~~~~~~~~~

There is no doubt that the time spent with my mother during the last ten weeks of her life has been rich with experiences, insights and lessons, some of which I have shared with you.

I also know that it changed me as a parent. I didn't want my children to ever feel alone or abandoned like I had felt with my mother. I wanted them to know that I would always be there for them, that I would show up for them because that was what was important and it was what mattered most.

In making the decision to be with Mom, to stay with her until the end, I was showing them that I had to be there for her, to care for her and to not abandon her.

I also had to make the decision and then make the decision right.

There were many reasons that I could have used to stay not with her, including my own family and businesses back home. I had an internal struggle most of the time I was there, wondering if I had made the right decision to be with her.

But I also knew that I had to make the decision to show up for Mom, to be there for her, despite if in the past I had felt abandoned. It was the right thing to do and the other pieces would fall into place to make the decision right.

This is important to note. As you continue to simplify your life by keeping what you honor, cherish and love, you will be challenged to make decisions. Sometimes the people in your life may challenge you and other times you may be challenged by your own internal voice. Some decisions will come easier while others will be harder to make.

Remember your goals, your vision and the reason you are simplifying your life.

Is it for your family? To have more time together? To be connected?

Is it to get control of your spending and have more to care for you and your loved ones?

Are you looking for more internal peace, calm and joy?

Are you wanting to create lasting memories and an enduring legacy?

Knowing the purpose behind simplifying your life will help guide you to complete the process and maintain it for years to come.

I'd also like to offer a few more suggestions to help you complete the process.

1. Follow Your Plan

It can be overwhelming to focus on too many things at once. Remember when you were doing your walk-thru and you found so much stuff in one area. You may have thought to yourself, "How am I going to get through all of this?"

Truth is, when you bring your focus to what is most important, you begin to sift through the clutter with greater ease. Having smaller, more succinct objectives will alleviate the overwhelm and allow you to move forward through the process.

In chapter three *Your Purge Will Set You Free*, you completed the exercise about your goals and your vision for each area of your life using this concept. You were encouraged to note one goal you had for each category for the next 3-6 months.

To create your plan, go back to that list, pick the most important area of your life on which you'd like to focus, and begin to scale back the goal by month, and then by week, until you reach today. For each of the months, list the top three most important things you need to do to move forward towards your ultimate goal for the period you set. Then take those monthly goals and break them down to the top three by week.

Starting with the end in mind and working your way back to the present, you'll create your step-by-step plan that you'll be able to follow and it won't be a list of a thousand things to do. It will be a list of Top 3's that you can follow each day, one day at a time, one week at a time, until you reach your ultimate goal for the period set.

This concept works well in the home transition services we offer to clients and it also works with private clients who are working towards their life goals.

Jenna was an artist at heart. She was a busy mother and she and her husband worked long hours to support the family. When Jenna came to me for coaching she expressed her longing to paint. She felt like her husband didn't fully support her and that her goal was one that he did not share. She felt alone and exasperated.

Through a priority exercise similar to what we did in chapter three, it was evident that Jenna really wanted to paint as her

> *profession. Despite her husband's lack of support, it was obvious this was a desire, a yearning she could not ignore.*
>
> *Together we created a step-by-step plan using the Top 3 exercise and developed a plan she could implement, one day at a time and one week at a time which eventually led to her having a painting room in her home and the support of her husband.*
>
> *By taking small steps daily she reached her ultimate goal and is now a thriving artist with public art displays. She is extremely happy and she continues to follow her vision for her painting career.*

Jenna wasn't sure how she was going to make her goals a reality, especially when she didn't feel she had the support of her husband. By applying being clear about her priorities and working with the Top 3 exercise to create her plan focused on what she really wanted and what was most important to her, not only did she create the career she had dreamed of, she gained the support of her husband.

Which leads me to your next safety net to simplifying your life.

2. Have a Support Team and a Coach

One of the things that I absolutely adhere to is having a support team and a coach.

I have to say that when I was in the hospital with Mom, I had a great support team. From my husband and my children, to my siblings and their families, to my husband's family and our teams in our businesses, each support person contributed to my being able to be with Mom to get through those days and weeks with her. Without them, I could not have done it.

Since then, I have always had a coach to help me through my grief and my losses. I've hired trained professionals to get me through the toughest of times and darkest of days.

On a professional level, I could not do the work that I do without a coach or two. Running two businesses, managing multiple teams and working with hundreds of clients requires a village, as the saying goes. I'm not alone in what I do and you shouldn't be either.

When we are working with our clients in home transitions or home organizing projects, we know that many of them want to do a lot of the work on their own.

We encourage them to take initiative and do some things by themselves but we also advise them that they will have far greater success, in less time with a team of people who know what they are going through and can lead the way through the process.

"You don't have to do it alone" is a strong belief that I hold. Although wanting to do things on our own may be noble, it can be expensive, far more challenging and create more problems than it solves.

I'm sure you have your own personal experiences where you tried to do something on your own and the moment you brought in someone to support you or guide you, results came far easier and you were able to get through it far quicker.

Same thing applies here. As you are navigating creating a life of abundance with what matters most, you'll find yourself wanting to do certain things on your own, and that's fantastic.

The moment you find yourself struggling, feeling stuck or frustrated it's time to reach out.

Stuff will happen and despite your best efforts, you'll get off track and begin to spiral back into where you were before you started this process. Having a coach to guide you along the way will shorten the time it takes to reach your goals and it will increase your overall success.

Like in the world of sports, a coach helps you to strategize, guide you, plan with you and support you along the way. It ensures continual growth and progress down the path where you feel in charge and in control of your life.

As an example, if you feel you are starting to slip financially, call in a money coach or a financial advisor to help you get aligned again.

If you feel yourself slipping with your weight, your health and well-being call in a personal trainer, or visit a nutritionist or a naturopath.

If you feel you are not connecting with your loved ones like you used to, seek counseling or do something with your family to reengage them.

Whatever you do, don't navigate your life alone without the help and support of someone who has been there before you, who is trained to help you and who can see things that you cannot see yourself.

When we first meet an individual or a family for a home transition or a home organizing project, during our initial consultation they are often overwhelmed by the entire thought of downsizing, decluttering and moving. Because we have the experience and the expertise to help them, we can see the entire process unfold even when they can't. We can guide them and support them every step of the way.

I follow a similar process when I am working with my private clients as well, as mentioned earlier. My role is to help them move forward even when they don't see three steps in front of them. I can also see more in them than they do themselves. My role is to guide and support them through the steps to take to make their lives the best they can be.

You can reach out to professionals in your area. You can reach out to me through my website at www.pierretteraymond.com. Or you can reach out to a trusted family member or friend who has navigated this type of transition before.

You'll also want to share with those that are most supportive of you and what you are doing. There may be people in your life that will disagree with what you are doing. They may feel that having more stuff in life is what gains the greatest pleasure and is the definition of success. They may feel that you are being guided down a path that will lead to your unhappiness rather to your joy-filled and abundant life.

When this happens, you'll want to ask yourself if they are the ones you want to share this experience with. Establish your priorities, use your top three and have support resources to guide you along the way.

3. Track Your Progress

There will be times where you'll ask yourself how much further you have to go before you reach your ultimate goal. Having a process to track your progress with timelines and milestones will allow you the opportunity to look back at how far you have come and encourage you to keep moving forward.

Although it may seem too simple, we recommend using a binder system to track your progress. This will ensure all your notes, resources and progress are tracked in one place.

Put your goal sheets in one binder. Have your top three's by week/day in the binder. Keep notes of your steps forward. Add encouraging emails you receive, inspirational quotes and articles that are helpful. Take photos before, during and after and insert them in your binder.

You can use dividers, colorful markers and pens; the sky's the limit when it comes to how creative you can be with this accountability and tracking binder.

Every morning, use it as your compass for the day. In the evening, before shutting things down, note your progress, list challenges you faced and add all that was encouraging and positive. Ensure your Top 3 for the next day are listed so you can get those done. Use it to track the progress you are making and any hiccups you encounter.

The binder will serve you well during your journey.

When we work with clients in their home transition and home organizing projects, we keep track of their progress through pictures, notes, and our internal tracking sheets. They often forget how much they have accomplished along the way and having a record to showcase it to them during and following their transition is remarkably gratifying for them. They are always surprised by what they accomplished and they always say that they couldn't have done it without us. The truth is, they did it with our guidance and support, but they are the ones who own the praise.

Our role is to support their priorities of what is most important and guide them along the way. The before, during and after record of their journey provides them with the recognition and acknowledgement they deserve for their commitment and perseverance through it all.

And you can do it too!

From the very first chapter, you were encouraged to get very clear about what is truly important in your life, to know what your priorities are in all areas of your life and to be there for who and what is truly important.

You evaluated your values and you have begun to use them as your compass.

You've started to focus on what you truly want, what is important and you are beginning to see it all come together. You're seeing how this process is going to save you a lot of time, energy and money as you move forward in your life. You are creating a life of pure abundance and happiness all while simplifying it.

The amazing thing is when you know what you want, why you want it and why it is important you'll begin to find opportunities come your way that you didn't expect before. You'll have richer and more engaging relationships. You'll eat better, exercise because you want to and you'll feel healthier and happier. You'll also keep your spending in check. You'll save and invest money like you haven't before. You'll also sleep better because you'll have a plan based on life goals that are important and you'll know that you are working towards them one step at a time.

All around you'll be happier, healthier and wealthier. It will be a true life of abundance!

4. Honor What You Love

This strategy may help you from slipping back into your old ways. It's one we use with all of our clients. It's all about honoring what is truly important.

From your health, to your finances, to your relationships and career, to your home and your car and the people in your life – honor everything and everyone that is important to you and you'll never feel like you're missing out on anything.

> *I met Gertrude two years ago when she was 88 years young. She never married nor had any children.*
>
> *She called upon my services because she was considering moving into a retirement home. She wasn't sure if the time was right but she wanted to explore this option with me.*
>
> *I met her in her beautiful apartment facing the Gatineau Hills. She talked about her small garden on her balcony and the joy she has had living in her quaint two-bedroom apartment for more than thirty years.*
>
> *At 88, she was very active in the community and she loved to drive her car. She was witty and would talk to me about authors and poets that I had not heard of. I was truly in awe of this beautiful and amazing woman.*

Our tasks together were simply to go through her items. There was not much to sort or purge as she had only kept the things that mattered most to her.

She proudly displayed her fine art pieces, sharing with me the rich history of each item and what they had meant to her through the years.

I asked if she knew the value of her property and she did not. I suggested that we have her items appraised and she'd have a better idea how much her things were worth. I also suggested that we do a full inventory of all of her pieces so she could gift them to her many nieces and nephews whom she adored.

She loved the idea and within a couple of weeks, we met with the appraiser.

As the appraiser walked through Gertrude's home, she recognized many of the fine pieces. Immediately, she and Gertrude engaged in rich conversation about the pieces, the artists and the stories that accompanied them. I was in awe and watched the magic unfold.

The appraiser started rhyming off values. $10,000. $8,000. $500. Oh, and $30,000.

Gertrude and I would look at each other, surprised and thrilled at the same time. Gertrude had no idea her items carried such high monetary value.

It was clear to Gertrude and I that the inventory list we'd share with her nieces and nephews would not have their appraised values included during the selection process.

"Let's avoid any issues arising because of what some of your items are worth", I said to Gertrude.

"I was thinking the same thing", she said back to me, knowing that no matter how wonderful her family was, these kinds of things could bring out the worst in some.

My task was then to put photos of the entire collection, without appraised values, in a document that we emailed and mailed to her many nieces and nephews. They had two weeks to choose the items they wanted Aunt Gertrude to gift to them when she moved or when she passed away.

Everyone obliged and Gertrude had her master list, ready for her move or for her estate. She was thrilled and I couldn't be happier for her.

What I learned most about this experience is that Gertrude, despite having a very simple life, was wealthy beyond any means. She surrounded herself with what she absolutely loved, proudly displaying it and honoring it for what it meant to her.

Because she lived this way, she also had great financial wealth. She had accumulated less stuff throughout her life but invested her time, money and resources in things that mattered most to her.

She was living an abundant and very happy life.

I'm happy to report that Gertrude just celebrated her 90th birthday and still has not moved from her beautiful apartment. She and I meet regularly for tea and we talk about her future move, which she isn't quite ready to make.

Gertrude is such an inspiration to me. She has taught me so much during the past two years despite us having not moved her into a retirement residence.

Every time she shares her life stories with me, I'm reminded that it's not the stuff that matters. It really is honoring what is really important and special and living a life that is focused on that.

I had the honor and the privilege of being a guest in the home of Larry Winget (www.larrywinget.com) a few months ago. Larry is known as the Pitbull of Personal Development® and he has come from having a very successful career, to being bankrupt to now being a multi-millionaire.

When a group of entrepreneurs and I visited his home in Arizona, there was no mistaking who's home we were in. Every item had a purpose, an intention, and a very distinct meaning. Everything represented Larry, his family and his life.

There was not a single piece of junk in sight. Everything was intentional and proudly honored and displayed. Their home represented who they are, what was important to them and it was an amazing home to be in.

I toured the house several times, listening intently to Larry tell the stories of his stuff. Many had heard of the infamous boot room and it was a real treat to see the floor-to-ceiling display of colorful, personally designed cowboy boots, proudly showcased for us to see. What I appreciated most were the heartwarming stories of his dogs, his personally crafted art pieces, his love of Elvis, the Lone Ranger and so much more.

Every time I walked through the home I noticed something different. I was fascinated by the amount of stuff that he had without a sign of clutter. He honored what he loved and what was important to him.

Every home should be just like that. Your home, my home, should be just that, a place to represent who we are and showcase what is truly important to us.

Visiting Larry's home reminded me of the importance of that.

So, here's your chance to do the same. Look around and ask yourself if you have proudly displayed in your home and in your office what has the most value to you, what is most special and most important.

Let's look at some of the physical items you may have and what you can do to honor them:

- ☐ Hang art pieces that mean the most to you. Create an art wall or have a section in your home dedicated to the pieces that have the most value to you, financially and/or sentimentally. There are great decorating tips online that you can find by simply going to your favorite search engine and looking for "DIY art display ideas and tips".

- ☐ Showcase your most favorite pieces that were gifted to you from a loved one. If they do not have special meaning, it's ok to let them go. If they hold sentimental value, display them for you to see and to share with others.

- ☐ If you're unable to keep a piece of furniture or an item of sentimental value, take a photograph of it, frame it and display the photograph. You can also take photographs of all the pieces you are letting go and make an album of your experience and of these items. You'll continue to enjoy the items without them taking up the space.

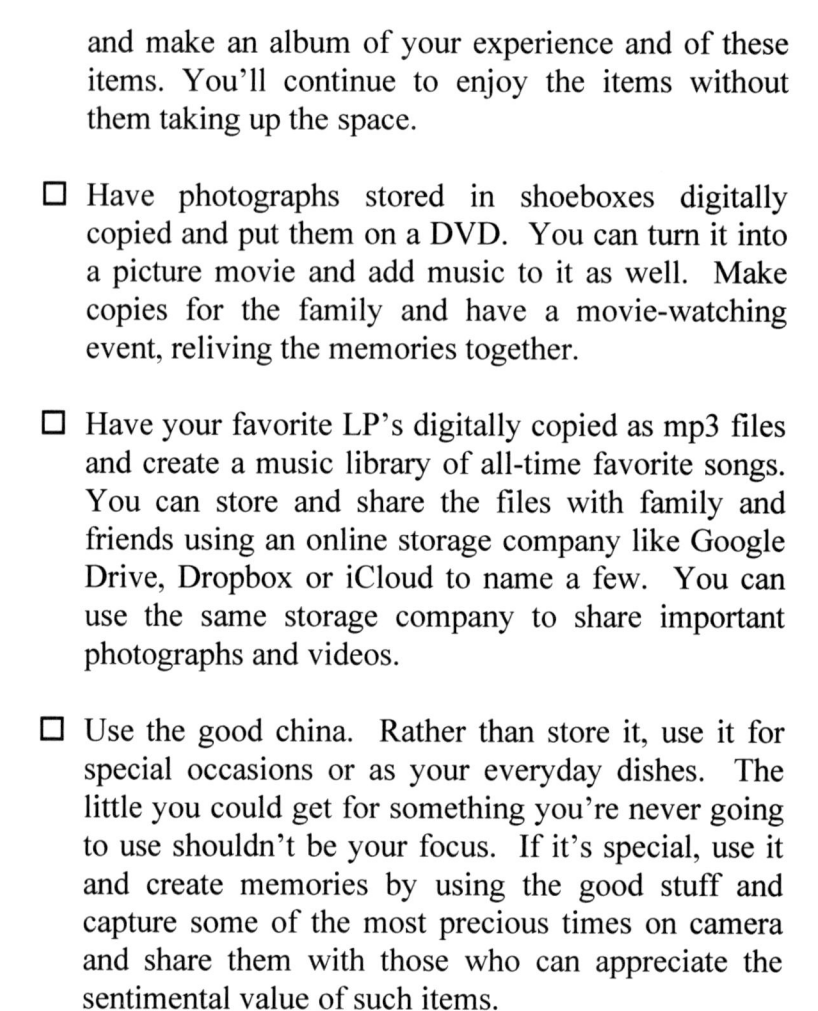

- ☐ Have photographs stored in shoeboxes digitally copied and put them on a DVD. You can turn it into a picture movie and add music to it as well. Make copies for the family and have a movie-watching event, reliving the memories together.

- ☐ Have your favorite LP's digitally copied as mp3 files and create a music library of all-time favorite songs. You can store and share the files with family and friends using an online storage company like Google Drive, Dropbox or iCloud to name a few. You can use the same storage company to share important photographs and videos.

- ☐ Use the good china. Rather than store it, use it for special occasions or as your everyday dishes. The little you could get for something you're never going to use shouldn't be your focus. If it's special, use it and create memories by using the good stuff and capture some of the most precious times on camera and share them with those who can appreciate the sentimental value of such items.

Honor what is in your life, that has meaning and that is special. Take care of what you value and showcase it, use it and display it.

When it comes to the other areas of your life, use the same principle.

Honor your health and wellbeing by caring for your body, taking time out to rest, to play and to rejuvenate.

Honor your money by tracking what you are spending, saving and earning. Donate to charities that mean something to you. Be very picky as to how you spend and save your money. Honor every penny by acknowledging it and using it for what matters most.

Your relationships are important. Honor them with quality time, loving conversations, and your attention. Send notes, surprise text messages and pick up the phone. Be attentive to those you love and be there when it matters most.

You'll find that when you choose to live your life making choices based on what is truly important, you'll eliminate far more of what you don't want and only keep what it is you truly want. You'll feel inspired, happy and far more fulfilled.

You may also begin to have another awareness. When you do bring stuff into your life that has little value, that upsets you or frustrates you, or that brings you down or makes you feel stuck, you'll immediately feel the shift.

You'll feel the weight of that stuff and it will drain you physically, emotionally and spiritually.

It's fascinating to experience and to watch.

So let it go. Let go of what is no longer serving you, what is no longer useful or important. Keep around you what you love and cherish most, and honor it.

5. **Your Legacy Matters**

Had I not had the experience with my mother, I probably wouldn't have the same awareness of legacy that I have now. She allowed me to assess our relationship, where we fell short, when we reconnected and how we maintained the love between us even during the last days of her life.

In addition, I'm very fortunate to have had clients in their seventies, eighties and nineties who bring an attentiveness to what matters most through their stories of joy and love, as well as their stories of regret and disappointment.

Imagine looking back on your life, as you prepare to celebrate your 95th birthday. Is it what you wanted it to be? Did you live your life honoring who and what was important? Did you show up for what mattered most?

I get to ask myself those questions every day through the amazing people I'm blessed to work with.

Honor your loved ones. Honor your stuff. Honor your life. Your legacy does matter and what you do today will affect the people that you love now and tomorrow.

In your life, remember to keep only what makes you feel great, what is really important, and you'll experience what it is like to have a full and abundant life.

"It doesn't matter where you are.
You are nowhere compared to where you can go."
Bob Proctor

It's your stuff. It's your story. It's your life.

APPENDIX

What Your Stuff Is Saying

~~~~

"Just play. Have fun. Enjoy the game."
Michael Jordan

~~~~

We've covered some pretty heavy stuff in this book, haven't we? And you stuck it through right to the end. Congratulations!

I wanted to add something fun that I wrote not too long ago. It's a quick reference guide that illustrates what our stuff may be saying about us.

There really is no right or wrong in this. It's just fun.

Perhaps when you completed your walk-thru and you noted what your stuff was saying about you, you may have found some interesting metaphors that got you to say "Hmmmmmm."

We find ourselves doing the same thing with every client. You just never know what message you will get when you start looking at your stuff from the perspective of what it may be saying to you and about you.

So to lighten things up a bit, as we close our time together here's a little resource to help you get through your stuff, now and in the future.

- **Books and magazines**: represent knowledge, experience, adventure and fun. Holding onto these could mean you crave adventure, you seek more knowledge or you want to learn and try new things. It also validates a sense of wisdom, intelligence and experience.

- **Baby items, kids crafts**: represent a special time when you were needed and loved unconditionally by your children. They symbolize a time of fun, joy and a special bond. You may be holding onto these items because you cherish the extraordinary bond you had with your children and you long to have that again. Plus, it's a direct connection to how much your children have grown.

- **Crafts, fabric, paints**: they represent the artistic, the creative, the adventurous. You may be craving to be just that again, carefree, creative and free-flowing. You may be feeling boxed-in by life and crave being set free.

- **Tools, and hardware**: these represent the do-it-yourself desire you have for projects in your life. You may be hanging on to those because you don't want to be caught unprepared for situations where you'll need to take care of repairs yourself. You may be missing projects that provide you a sense of accomplishment and personal growth.

- **Shoes, clothes, handbags**: they represent style, class and status. If you are hanging onto these items but are not using them, you may be living in the past where you felt like they represented who you were or who you desire to be. They no longer serve that purpose. You may be feeling frustrated and empty and you are holding onto them to feed a desire to be that person again.

- **Records (LP's), tapes, 8 tracks**: music bonds us to the memories of our lives. Play a song and you relive the memory instantly. Holding onto the music means

holding onto the memories. You may be lacking new experiences that enrich your life. You may be feeling like the past was the best time of your life and the music of the past brings it all back to you in the present.
- **Photographs**: the snapshots of our lives. Holding onto them means holding onto and preserving all of your memories. Holding onto to all of them, even when they are not important may mean you do not want to let go for fear that you'll miss something from your past. You may be missing the good old days.

- **Papers**: they connect us to information, to what is important to document and keep. By keeping too much paper, you are not making decisions on what is truly important to have in your life. Everything seems important and you can't let it go. You may be missing a clear definition of what you believe is important in your life. You may be feeling scattered and overwhelmed.

As with everything, knowing what is really important will help you to let go of that which is not important.

It can also open your eyes to things you may be missing in your life.

Sometimes it's just a matter of awareness and big improvements can be made. Other times, real conscious effort is necessary to look at the stuff and decide how it is either holding you back or keeping you stuck.

When you are able to view the items as "stuff" that is either important, holding you back, or keeping you stuck, you'll be able to decide what to do with it.

It's also a fun way to look at where you are in your life so you can decide if it's time to spice it up, be more adventurous and curious, and really begin to live life fully.

It's your stuff. It's your story. It's your life!

Here's to making it the best it can be!

BIBLIOGRAPHY

The following sources were quoted in the book. I did my best to cite the original source however some quoted resources may be referenced through organization and association websites. I have provided website addresses to allow the referenced material to be found.

Chapter Three

1. Herr, Norman PhD, (2008). *The Sourcebook for Teaching Science.* John Wiley & Sons, Inc. Jossey-Bass.

2. Annenberg Center for Digital Future, University of Southern California. (2008). www.annenber.usc.edu.

3. MacKenzie Neal, Richard, (2009). *The Long Road Home...A Philosophical Journey.* AuthorHouse. P.86.

4. Center for the Prevention of School-Aged Violence (2010). Online at http://goodwin.drexel.edu/cposav/sav_stats.php; National Education Association, http://www.nea.org.

5. Bullying Statistics, (2010). Online at www.bullyingstatistics.org.

6. Cassada Lohmann, Rachell, MS, LPC, (2012). *Surviving Bullying.* Psychology Today. Online at http://www.psychologytoday.com/blog/teen-angst/201209/surviving-bullying.

7. American Association of Suicidology (2010). Online at http://www.suicidology.org.

8. Kim, Young-Shin, M.D, (2008). Yale School of Medicine: Child Study Center. Online at http://news.yale.edu/2008/07/16/bullying-suicide-link-explored-new-study-researchers-yale.

9. American Association of Suicidology, (2010). Online at http://www.suicidology.org.

10. Costello EJ, Mustillo S, Erkanli A et al. (2003). *Prevalence and development of psychiatric disorders in childhood and adolescence.* Arch Gen Psychiatry.

11. Substance Abuse and Mental Health Services Administration, National Survey on Drug Use & Health (2012). *Depression rates triple between the ages of 12 and 15 among adolescent girls.* Online at http://www.samhsa.gov/data/spotlight/Spot077GirlsDepression2012.pdf

12. U.S. Department of Health and Human Services, (1999). Mental Health: A Report of the Surgeon General. Rockville, Md., U.S. Department of Health and Human Services, Substance Abuse and Mental Health Services Administration, Center for Mental Health Services.

13. National Alliance on Mental Health, (n.d). Depression in Children & Adolescent Fact Sheet. Online at http://www.nami.org/Template.cfm?Section=Depression&Template=/ContentManagement/ContentDisplay.cfm&ContentID=89198

14. Eisenberg, Marla E., ScD, MPH; Olson, Rachel E., MS; Neumark-Sztainer, Dianne, PhD, MPH, RD; Story, Story, PhD, RD; Bearinger, Linda H., PhD, MS, (2004). *Correlations Between Family Meals and Psychosocial*

Well-being Among Adolescents. Archives of Pediatric & Adolescent Medicine. Online at http://archpedi.jamanetwork.com/article.aspx?articleid=485781.

15. Mason Kiefer, Heather, (2004). *Empty Seats: Fewer Families Eat Together.* Gallop Poll. Online at http://www.gallup.com/poll/10336/empty-seats-fewer-families-eat-together.aspx.

Chapter Five

16. Bretherton, Inge (1992). *The Origins of Attachment Theory: John Bowlby and Mary Ainsworth.* Online at http://www.psychology.sunysb.edu/attachment/online/inge_origins.pdf

17. Institue of Medicine, (2012). *Measuring Progress in Obesity Prevention.* Online at http://www.iom.edu/Reports/2012/Measuring-Progress-in-Obesity-Prevention.aspx

18. Jakes, T.D, (2012). *Commitment.* Online at http://www.youtube.com/watch?v=n04Bf85mLZU and http://www.youtube.com/watch?v=AS5MM5C8pzU.

19. Byock, Ira, MD, (2004). *The Four Things That Matter Most.* Atria Books.

ABOUT THE AUTHOR

For more than thirteen years, Pierrette Raymond has helped families and individuals get through some of life's toughest moments. Whether they are moving, downsizing or decluttering their spaces, going through a major life transition, or the loss of a loved one, Pierrette's role has always been one of comfort, support and guidance to help them get unstuck, let go and move forward.

With a background in psychology and education, a masters in NLP (Neuro-Linguistic Programming) and subsequent training in death, dying, bereavement, grief recovery as well as certifications as a Relocation and Transition Specialist, Pierrette is a woman who understands the challenges people face following major life transitions including moving, death & loss and aging.

She lives in Ottawa, Ontario with her husband, two children and two dogs.

For more information about Pierrette, vist her website at www.pierretteraymond.com.

CPSIA information can be obtained at www.ICGtesting.com
Printed in the USA
LVOW121917180613

339219LV00008B/39/P